To the many students we have had the pleasure of teaching over the years, for the inspiration their many questions have provided.

Contents

Idioms	Conversations	Ten-Minute Grammar Games
Hi. Nice to meet you. I'm pleased to meet you. How's it going? Okay. Not bad. Pretty good. How about you?	Nice to Meet You How's It going?	Back and Forth Getting Together
I've got to go now. Have a nice day. You too. Pretty cold weather, eh? It's freezing. Yeah.	I've Got To Go Now It's Freezing Today	Mystery Person Back and Forth
picture kids What a nice family! Hurry up! over there right here Let's go.	What a Nice Family! Hurry Up, We're late!	The Question Game Chain Find Someone
Sorry. Thanks. 'Bye. You have the wrong number. Excuse me. No problem.	Can I Leave My Number? Sorry, Wrong Number	I Spy Mystery Person Find Someone

Idioms	Conversations	Ten-Minute Grammar Games
It's too small. Thanks anyway. I've got place What's it like? Thanks a lot.	Do You Have an Apartment for Rent? I've Got A New Place	Mystery Objects Mystery Person Mystery Box
get it over there No problem Me too. Do You Want a Lift?	Does This Bus Go Downtown? Do You Want a Lift?	Back and Forth I Spy Find Someone
Is _____ there please? Speaking. This is _____. Nothing special. I need a rest. Boy! So so.	What Did You Do Yesterday? How Was Your Weekend?	Chain Back and Forth
terrible How come? mad That's too bad. That's lucky.	Late for Work A Terrible Day	Mystery Box The Question Game
What's for supper? heat it up Is there anything else? What a (great party)! Let's try (the chicken). I'm starving Come on.	What's for Supper? What a Great Party!	Any Suggestions? Mystery Box

Idioms	Conversations	Ten-Minute Grammar Games
on special Does it come in (blue)? You're welcome. What's up? right now we can get together It sounds good.	I'm Looking for a Jacket What Are You Doing Today?	Charades Memory I Spy
not much not really I love (it). How was it? pretty boring How come? That's too bad	What Were You Doing Yesterday? How Was the Party?	Charades What's the Reason?
sleep in nah take it easy Any plans? Who knows? come on over a friend of mine	What Are You Going to Do on the Weekend? This Is a Friend of Mine	Mystery Box Chain
Appendix 3 Page 204 Wh- Questions and Answers Simple Aspect, Continuous Aspect Imperatives **Let's** for Suggestions Past Tense Irregular Verbs		

To the Teacher

Grammar Connections provides clear, systematic coverage of basic grammatical structures. It is geared towards students who are beginners in English, as well as students who need to complement their language development with attention to accuracy.

The units of the book use a carefully controlled lexicon so as not to detract from the focus on structure. Each one follows a sequence of activities that takes students through several steps.

To begin, new vocabulary is presented visually in a section called "Words You Need." This is followed by "Understanding Grammar," a section that includes explanations and comprehensive practice exercises. "Listening and Speaking: Using Idioms" presents the real language that people use every day. The taped dialogues deal with some common difficulties in using social language, and bridge the gap between formal classroom learning and real-life language. Realistic conversations allow students to practise common idiomatic expressions that follow up and build on structures from the units. For example, the formal greeting "How are you?" is complemented with the idiomatic greeting "How's it going?" in the taped dialogues.

Through these three sections, a picture dictionary runs across the bottom of each page to provide an instant reference for new vocabulary. These clear graphic illustrations also support general language development.

The "Ten-Minute Grammar Games" that are included in every unit provide a variety of simple, easy-to-play games as a lively way to practise the structures that have been taught. Teachers and students will appreciate activities that involve everyone in a few minutes of fun at the end of a grammar lesson.

Each unit concludes with activities that allow students to test and monitor their own progress. Every fifth unit provides a review of the structures and vocabulary of the preceding four units. Answer keys to all the exercises are included at the back of the book.

Acknowledgements

We would like to express our appreciation to colleagues and administrators at l'Université de Montréal, O'Sullivan College and Language Studies Canada. Thanks go to Johanne Rousseau, Wendy Thatcher, Yvonne Saleh, Mary Strong, Mary Tomaras, Daniel Boulerice, and Maxime Cutler at O'Sullivan College and to the following students who participated in the final testing of the materials: Maria-Elena Alvarez, Lise Bergeron, Francine Cloutier, Francine Tremblay, Renée Rivard, Alala Benboudadi, and Nadia Saim. We would also like to thank Diane St. Jean for her help in proofreading.

We are grateful for the superb professionalism and invaluable collaboration of our editors Elynor Kagan and Marta Tomins. We are also grateful for our association with many fine professionals: Kedre Murray, Joe March, Cliff Newman, Joe Chin and Jan Elliot. We would like to extend our appreciation to Yolanda de Rooy for inspiring this project and continuing to offer advice and support.

Our thanks go also to our families for their love and patience. Special thanks to Max and Millicent Goldman for their acuity in proofreading the final manuscript, and for their unflagging encouragement in so many ways over the years.

1

Subject Pronouns
Verb "Be"
Plural Nouns

Subject Pronouns

I
you
he
she
it

we
you
they

"Be" Affirmative

I am
you are
he is
she is
it is

we are
you are
they are

Contraction

I'm
you're
he's
she's
it's

we're
you're
they're

Words You Need

A. 1. Practise with the teacher.

2. Practise with a partner.

Anne: Hello, I am Anne Martin. I'm from Montreal.

Max: Hello, I'm Max Kuslov. I'm from Moscow.

Yumi: Hello, I am Yumi Suzuki. I'm from Kyoto.

Carla: Hi, I am Carla Lopez, and this is Roberto Lopez. We are from Mexico City.

Tom: Hi, I'm Tom Kirk. I'm from Los Angeles.

Chen: Hello, I am Chen Han. This is Lili Han. We're from Hong Kong.

Ali: Hello, we are Ali and Nadia Aziz. We're from Cairo.

Joseph: Hi, I'm Joseph Muna. I'm from Youandé.

Anne Martin

Tom Kirk

Lili Han   Chen Han

Max Kuslov

Yumi Suzuki

Nadia Aziz   Ali Aziz

Carla Lopez   Roberto Lopez   Joseph Muna

B. Answer **yes** or **no**.

1. Mr. Kirk is from the United States.
2. Mr. Han is from Shanghai.
3. Ms. Suzuki is from Tokyo.
4. Mr. and Mrs. Lopez are from Madrid.
5. Ms. Martin is from Montreal.
6. Mr. and Mrs. Han are from Hong Kong.
7. Mr. Muna is from New York.
8. Mrs. Lopez is from Los Angeles.
9. Mr. Kuslov is from Moscow.
10. Nadia Aziz is from Cairo.

Language in Transition: Titles	
Mr. (mister)	for a man
Ms. (miz)	for a woman
Mrs. (missus)	for a married woman
Miss	for an unmarried woman
Ms. is a modern title for women in business or professions.	

Understanding Grammar

UNDERSTAND: **Greetings**

Look at the pictures and greetings.

Right: ✔ Hi, Tom.
       ✔ Hello, Mr. Kirk.

Right: ✔ Hi, Yumi.
       ✔ Hello, Ms. Suzuki.

Right: ✔ Hi, Anne.
       ✔ Hello, Ms. Martin.
       ✔ Good morning, Dr. Martin.

Wrong: ✘ Hello, Ms. Yumi.
       ✘ Hello, Dr. Anne.
       ✘ Hello, Mr. Tom.

Wrong: ✘ Hello, teacher.
       ✘ Hello, Mr. Teacher.
       ✘ Hello, Mrs. Teacher.
       ✘ Hello, my teacher.

Say: **Hi, Tom.**
Hello, Mr. Kirk.

Say: **Hi, Yumi.**
Hello, Ms. Suzuki.

Say: **Hi, Ann.**
Hello, Ms. Martin.
Hello, Dr. Martin.

a man

a woman

a teacher

students

a classroom

a greeting

A. Look at the pictures on page 2. Write a greeting for each person.

B. 1. Write a greeting for your teacher.
    2. Write a greeting for you.

C. Greet students in the class. Say your name:

    Hello, I'm (first name, family name).
    Hi (first name or title and family name).

> **Language in Transition**
>
> **Hi** is a common informal greeting. **Hello** is more formal. **Good morning** or **Good afternoon** are for formal or very polite situations.

UNDERSTAND: **Subject Pronouns**

Look at the pictures.

TEACHER'S BOX: The English pronoun system uses many irregular and inconsistent forms and can be difficult for students. Here are some particular points to mention about subject pronouns:

he = male
she = female
it   = things, animals
they = plural for males, females, animals or things

a doctor   a person   people   first name   family name   a door

A. Find the pronouns. Show the nouns.

The people are at the airport. (They) are passengers. A man is near the counter. He is Mr. Kuslov from Moscow. A woman is near the suitcases. She is Carla Lopez from Mexico City. Two people are near the door. They are Mr. and Mrs. Han from Hong Kong.

B. Write the pronoun:

Mrs. Han   **she**

1. a woman
2. passengers
3. people
4. Carla Lopez
5. Mr. Kuslov

6. a man
7. Mr. and Mrs. Han
8. Roberto Lopez
9. Mr. Kirk
10. Nadia Aziz

near   far   airport   passengers   a counter   suitcases

C.   Which pronouns are wrong? Correct wrong pronouns.

1. Yumi is from Kyoto. He is a teacher.
2. Anne Martin is from Montreal. It is a doctor.
3. Tom and Roberto are tall. They are friends.
4. Roberto and Carla are tourists. She are from Mexico.
5. Lili is from Hong Kong. She is a bank teller.
6. Ali and Nadia Aziz are near the door. They are from Cairo.
7. The suitcase is near the counter. They is big.
8. Carla and Yumi are women. She are friends.
9. Lili and Chen are from Hong Kong. They are tourists.
10. The people are at the airport. It are passengers.

UNDERSTAND: **Verb "Be"**

Use **be** in sentences with no action:

I am	we are
you are	you are
he is	they are
she is	
it is	
you are	

He is Max.
He is tall.
He is Russian.

Use the verb **be** with:

Names	**Age**	**Jobs**	**Nationality**
I am Anne.	He is ten years old.	I am a student.	I am Mexican.
She is Yumi.	She is two.	They are teachers.	He is Japanese.
Location	**Description**	**Emotions**	
They are from Bolivia.	He is old.	We are happy.	
It is in the hotel.	She is tall.	They are tired.	

tall/short   tourists   friends   a bank teller   big   small

A. Write the verb.

1. The woman _____ from Canada.
2. The hotel _____ new.
3. The girls _____ friends.
4. Toronto _____ in Canada.
5. I _____ a student.
6. Maria _____ from Mexico.
7. The rooms _____ small.

> **TEACHER'S BOX:** Many languages use the verb **be** differently. For example, some languages use **have** for age. Students new to English will use the forms of their own languages.

8. The man _____ tall.
9. Tom and I _____ tourists.
10. The bus _____ big.

B. Write the verb.

1. He _____ near the desk.
2. We _____ tourists.
3. You _____ tall.
4. I _____ from Japan.
5. She _____ short.
6. They _____ Spanish.
7. He _____ 27 years old.
8. They _____ happy.
9. We _____ students.
10. You _____ tired.

C. Which sentences are wrong? Correct wrong verbs.

1. The friends be happy.
2. He are 19 years old.
3. The suitcase is old.
4. I be from Russia.
5. You is 26 years old.
6. We are friends.
7. The woman is tall.
8. The airport be big.
9. They are tourists.
10. We be tired.

UNDERSTAND: **Plural Nouns**

Use **s** after a noun for the plural form:

1 student   3 students

Exceptions: person   people
man   men
woman   women
child   children

> **Language in Transition**
>
> The plural form of **person** can be **persons**, but it is more usual in current English to use **people** as the plural form.

a hotel   a bus   happy   tired   new   old

8

A. Write the plurals.

1. teacher
2. tourist
3. child
4. person
5. suitcase
6. room

7. name
8. camera
9. woman
10. job
11. doctor
12. student

13. man
14. airport
15. girl
16. mother

B. Which sentences are wrong? Correct the wrong plurals.

1. Nancy and Anne are woman.
2. The childrens are in the lobby.
3. There are two hotel on the street.
4. Ali and Tom are friends.
5. We are tourist from Mexico.

6. Pedro is a children.
7. They are old suitcase.
8. The two women are strong.
9. Three peoples are in the taxi.
10. The rooms are small.

UNDERSTAND: **Verb "Be" Contraction**

Contractions are short forms for speaking and for informal writing:

Hi, I'm from China.
This is my friend. He's from France.

Full Form	Contraction	TEACHER'S BOX: Contractions are used in speaking and less formal writing. The apostrophe should not be confused with the comma. Students not familiar with Western script may need practice writing apostrophes above the line.
I am	I'm	
you are	you're	
he is	he's	
she is	she's	
it is	it's	
we are	we're	
you are	you're	
they are	they're	

a girl   a boy   a child   children   a mother   a father

A. Write the letter represented by the apostrophe (′):

we're: **a** (we are)

1. they're
2. he's
3. you're
4. it's
5. we're
6. I'm
7. she's

B. Write the contraction of the verb.

1. _____ 24 years old. (She is)
2. _____ from the United States. (I am)
3. _____ a doctor. (He is)
4. _____ Canadian. (You are)
5. _____ tourists. (We are)
6. _____ tall. (He is)
7. _____ in the airport. (They are)
8. _____ friends. (You are)

> **TEACHER'S BOX:** See the reference list of countries and nationalities in Appendix 1 (page 200). Students may confuse country and nationality, and say sentences such as, "She's the China girl" instead of "She's the Chinese girl."

Listening and Speaking: Using Idioms

Nice to Meet You

A. Practise the expressions with the teacher.

Hello.	= **Hi.**
It is nice to meet you.	= **Nice to meet you.**
I am happy to meet you.	= **I'm pleased to meet you.**

a camera　　a job　　a taxi　　a desk　　a lobby　　strong

B. Listen and write the words.

Conversation 1

Nadia: Hello. My name is Nadia. I'm from Egypt.

Anne: _____ Nadia. Nice to meet you. _____ Anne. I'm from Canada.

Nadia: _____ pleased to meet you, Anne.

Anne: I'm pleased _____ meet you too, Nadia.

Conversation 2

Tom: Hello. I'm Tom. I'm _____ the United States.

Yumi: Hi Tom. _____ to meet you. My name is Yumi.

Tom: Are you from Japan, Yumi?

Yumi: Yes, _____ from Kyoto, Japan.

Tom: I'm pleased to _____ you.

C. Practise the conversations with a partner.

How's It Going?

A. Practise the expressions with the teacher.

How are you?	= **How's it going?**
I'm fine.	= **Okay. Not bad. Pretty good.**
And you, how are you?	= **How about you?**

B. Listen and write the words.

Max: Hi. How's _____ going, Ali?

Ali: Okay. How _____ you, Max?

Max: Pretty good. _____ your new job?

Ali: _____ bad. It's a good job.

C. Practise the conversation with a partner.

Suggestions

Practise the conversations. Memorize one conversation. Act it out for the class.

a country   a city   an address   a phone number   an apartment number

Ten-Minute Grammar Games

Back and Forth

Focus: Practise the verb **be** affirmative and negative. Practise subject pronouns.

This game also helps students learn the names of their classmates. It can be done with the whole class or in groups.

1. The teacher begins by saying, "I am Yumi." The students respond by saying: "No, you're not. You are the teacher."

2. A student takes over and says, "I am ___." If the student gives his or her correct name, the class responds by saying, "Yes, you are." If the name is incorrect, students respond by saying, "No, you're not. You're ___."

3. After one round of each student saying his or her own name, students name each other. For example, a student begins by saying, "He is Amir." Other students answer, "Yes, he is" or "No, he isn't; he's Roberto." Then Roberto continues by identifying another student, until everyone has been named.

4. Continue naming students, using different pronouns—for example, "They are Nancy and Patrick." The students respond, "Yes, we are" or "No, we're not. We're Nancy and George."

Getting Together

Focus: Practise introductions. Meet classmates.

1. Students work in pairs, introducing themselves:

   Hi. I'm Henry. Nice to meet you.
   Hello, I'm Janet. Nice to meet you too.

2. Students work with new partners to practise again.

3. Students walk around the room, shaking hands and meeting each other.

4. When they have finished, they can work in groups of three or four and take turns introducing students in the group:

   This is Amir. This is Janet.

Test Yourself

Meeting and Greeting

A. Choose the answer.

1. Mr. Han is
   a) a man
   b) a woman

2. "Anne" and "Roberto" are
   a) first names
   b) last names

3. Japanese is
   a) a language
   b) a country

4. A good greeting is
   a) Hello, Dr. Anne.
   b) Hello, Dr. Martin.

5. Miss Green is
   a) a woman
   b) a man

6. "Pretty good" =
   a) bad
   b) very good

7. A good greeting is
   a) Hello, Mrs. Jones.
   b) Hello, Mrs. Teacher.

8. "How's it going?" =
   a) "How are you?"
   b) "Where are you going?"

B. Match questions and answers.

How are you?   Fine, thanks.

1. Nice to meet you, Bob.
2. Family name, please?
3. Is the weather good?
4. Are you from Italy?
5. Is he strong?
6. Is she 21 years old?

a) Yes. I am.
b) Pleased to meet you.
c) No, she's 24.
d) Suzuki.
e) Yes, it is.
f) Yes, he is.

Verb "Be"

A. Write the verb **be** (**is, am, are**).

1. We _____ tourists.
2. Yumi _____ a teacher.
3. I _____ 20 years old.
4. Anne and Guy _____ French.
5. We _____ tired.

6. He _____ 40 years old.
7. Osaka _____ a city in Japan.
8. Carla and Roberto _____ from Mexico.
9. China _____ a big county.
10. The children _____ happy.

B. Write the sentences. Use contractions:

They are tall.   **They're** tall.

1. He is American.
2. We are from Spain.
3. I am happy to meet you.
4. She is a child.
5. I am 18 years old.

6. They are friends
7. He is 26.
8. It is late.
9. We are tourists.
10. She is short.

Subject Pronouns (I, you, he, she, it, we, they)

Write the pronoun:

Joe is big. **He** is strong.

1. Lili is a woman. _____ is from Hong Kong.
2. Ali and Nadia are tourists. _____ are from Egypt.
3. The suitcase is in the lobby._____ is heavy.
4. Hi, my name is Yumi. _____ am from Japan.
5. Max is Russian. _____ is a mechanic.
6. Nice to meet you, Chen. Where are _____ from?
7. _____ am pleased to meet you.
8. Yumi is young. _____ is 24 years old.
9. Yumi and Anne are women. _____ are friends.
10. Hello, Max and Tony. _____ are late.

Vocabulary

A. One word is wrong. Find the word.

1. doctor   student   woman   teller   teacher
2. bus   job   airport   hotel   tourist
3. name   age   nationality   Peru   job
4. strong   happy   tired   friend   young
5. Egyptian   Russian   China   Spanish   French

B. Write the plural.

1. woman
2. friend
3. student
4. child
5. doctor

6. person
7. tourist
8. room
9. man
10. teacher

C. Complete the conversations.

1. Hello, my _____ is Maria. I am _____ Italy. I am Italian. My _____ name is Rossi. I am 20 years _____.

2. **Nadia:** Hello. I'm Nadia.

   Yumi: Hi, Nadia. Nice to _____ you. I'm Yumi.

   Nadia: Nice to meet you, Yumi. Are you _____ Japan?

   Yumi: Yes. _____ are you from Nadia?

   Nadia: I'm from Egypt. I'm _____.

3.   **Joseph:** Hi. How's it _____, Max?

     Max: Not _____. How are you, Joseph?

     Joseph: Pretty _____. How's your new job?

     Max: Okay.

2

Verb "Be": Question Form, Negative Form
Short Answers
Special Uses of "It is"

Affirmative

I am	we are
you are	you are
he is	they are
she is	
it is	

Question

am I	are we
are you	are you
is he	are they
is she	
is it	

?

Negative

I am not	we are not
you are not	you are not
he is not	they are not
she is not	
it is not	

Contraction A

I'm not	we're not
you're not	you're not
he's not	they're not
she's not	
it's not	

Contraction B

	we aren't
you aren't	you aren't
he isn't	they aren't
she isn't	
it isn't	

Words You Need

Family name	Martin
First name	Anne
Nationality	Canadian
Age	26 years old
Occupation (job)	doctor

Family name	Kirk
First name	Tom
Nationality	American
Age	34 years old
Occupation (job)	flight attendant

Family name	Kuslov
First name	Max
Nationality	Russian
Age	19 years old
Occupation (job)	mechanic

Read the cards. Write **Yes** or **No**:

Anne Martin is French.   **No**

1. Tom is Japanese.
2. Max is 19 years old.
3. Max is a mechanic.
4. Anne is Canadian.

5. Tom is a teacher.
6. Anne is 24 years old.
7. Tom is 34 years old.
8. Anne is a doctor.

TEACHER'S BOX: When describing a person's nationality, the indefinite article **a** or **an** is generally omitted. When describing a person's occupation, the indefinite article **a** or **an** is required:

She is Canadian. She is **a** doctor.
Wrong   ✗ She is doctor.
Right   ✔ She is **a** doctor.

Understanding Grammar

UNDERSTAND: **"Be" Question Form**

Put the verb before the subject for a question with **be**. Put a question mark (**?**) at the end of a question:

Are they tourists?

Affirmative	
I am	we are
you are	you are
he is	they are
she is	
it is	

Question		
am I	are we	
are you	are you	**?**
is he	are they	
is she		
is it		

A. Write a question:

She is Canadian.   **Is she Canadian?**

1. They are Taiwanese.
2. Mr. Lopez is Spanish.
3. She is a teacher.
4. We are tourists. (Use **you**)
5. Yumi is Japanese.
6. Tom is American.
7. She is a doctor.
8. I am late.
9. Nadia Aziz is an engineer.
10. They are happy.

| early | late | a flight attendant | a pilot | a mechanic |

B. Write five questions about the people. Use the information below.

Is Yumi Japanese?

Family name	Suzuki	Family name	Han
First name	Yumi	First name	Chen
Nationality	Japanese	Nationality	Chinese
Age	24	Age	31
Occupation (job)	teacher	Occupation (job)	photographer
	Family name	Aziz	
	First name	Nadia	
	Nationality	Egyptian	
	Age	25	
	Occupation (job)	engineer	

UNDERSTAND: **"Be" Negative**

Add **not** after the verb for a negative statement with **be**:

They are **not** students.

Affirmative	
I am	we are
you are	you are
he is	they are
she is	
it is	

Negative	
I am not	we are not
you are not	you are not
he is not	they are not
she is not	
it is not	

A. Write the negative:

We are English.   We are **not** English.

1. I am Canadian.
2. He is American.
3. They are Japanese.
4. She is French.
5. We are Korean.

6. She is Australian.
7. He is Italian.
8. They are Turkish.
9. She is Chinese.
10. They are Brazilian.

a photograph   a photographer   an engineer   an airplane   a pencil   a pen

B. Write the word:

I _____ not English.   I **am** not English.

1. Mr. Aziz is _____ Moroccan.
2. _____ am not American.
3. Chen _____ not Japanese.
4. Dr. Martin is _____ Australian.
5. We _____ not Italian.

6. They are _____ Chinese.
7. I _____ not French.
8. He is _____ Canadian.
9. They _____ not Lebanese.
10. She _____ not Greek.

UNDERSTAND: **"Be" Contraction**

Use the contraction (short form) of the verb **be** + **not** for speaking or informal writing. Look at two forms of the negative contraction.

Full Form	
I am not	we are not
you are not	you are not
he is not	they are not
she is not	
it is not	

Contraction A	
I'm not	we're not
you're not	you're not
he's not	they're not
she's not	
it's not	

Contraction B	
	we aren't
you aren't	you aren't
he isn't	they aren't
she isn't	
it isn't	

TEACHER'S BOX: There are two ways to form the negative contraction with **be**. They are interchangeable. The exception is the first person singular which has only one negative form.

A. Write the contraction. Use Contraction Form A:

we are not: **we're not**

1. I am not
2. he is not
3. you are not

4. it is not
5. they are not
6. she is not

a bus driver   a taxi driver   a cat   a clock   students   tourists

B. Look at the example. Write a negative sentence. Use a subject pronoun and the word in brackets ( ):

Nancy is from Mexico. (Peru) **She isn't from Peru.**

1. Yumi is Japanese. (Chinese)
2. The airport is big. (small)
3. The tourists are American. (French)
4. I'm in North America. (England)
5. My friends and I are students. (tourists)
6. Max is a mechanic. (a bus driver)
7. Tom is a flight attendant. (an engineer)
8. Pedro is five years old. (six years old)
9. You are American. (Canadian)
10. The cat is small. (big)

UNDERSTAND: **"Be" Short Answers**

Use **yes** or **no** + subject and verb to answer questions. It is not necessary to answer with a sentence when you speak.

Look at the pictures. Choose the answers.

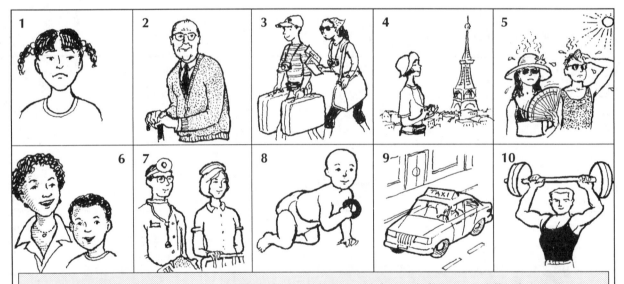

TEACHER'S BOX: Forming short answers with the subject and the verb **be** is not difficult. However, students may find it strange to use the subject and **be** without a complement. They need to look carefully at the examples:

Question: Is she happy?   Short Answer: **Yes, she is.** (happy)

worried   sad   hungry   thirsty   hot   cold

You are late.   Yes, we are.   (No, we aren't.)

1. She's sad.	Yes, she is.	No, she isn't.
2. He is 18 years old.	Yes, he is.	No, he isn't.
3. They're students.	Yes, they are.	No, they aren't.
4. I'm in France.	Yes, you are.	No, you aren't.
5. We're hot.	Yes, you are.	No, you aren't.
6. They are happy.	Yes, they are.	No, they aren't.
7. You are tourists.	Yes, we are.	No, we aren't.
8. She is 6 years old.	Yes, she is.	No, she isn't.
9. He is a taxi driver.	Yes, he is.	No, he isn't.
10. You're strong.	Yes, I am.	No, I'm not.

UNDERSTAND: **Special Uses of "It is"**

Use **It is** for time:

It is three o'clock.

It is early.

Use **It is** for days and dates:

It is Monday.

It is July 21st.

Use **It is** for weather.

Affirmative: **It is** hot today.

Question: **Is it** cold in Canada?

Is it cold in Indonesia?

Short answer: Yes, it is.   No, it isn't.

TEACHER'S BOX: See Appendix 1 (page 199) for a list of ordinal numbers, cardinal numbers, and a list of seasons. See Appendix 2 (page 202) for clock faces, days of the week, and months.

warm   cool   windy   snowy   rainy   sunny

A. Look at the clocks. Say the times.

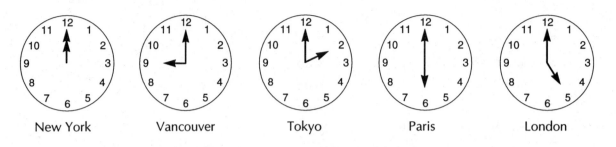

| New York | Vancouver | Tokyo | Paris | London |

Language in Transition

People often give the time as two numbers:

It's 10:20.   It's ten twenty.

B. Match the questions and answers.

1. What time is it?   a) It's Monday.
2. What day is it?   b) It's April 15.
3. What's the date?   c) It's spring.
4. What month is it?   d) It's 3:10.
5. What season is it?   e) It's September.
6. What year is it?   f) It's 19____.

C. Look at the map on page 23. Answer the questions.

1. Is it hot in Moscow?   Yes, it is.   No, it isn't.
2. Is it warm in Anchorage?   Yes, it is.   No, it isn't.
3. Is it cold in Stockholm?   Yes, it is.   No, it isn't.
4. Is it cold in Cairo?   Yes, it is.   No, it isn't.
5. Is it cool in Tokyo?   Yes, it is.   No, it isn't.
6. Is it hot in Buenos Aires?   Yes, it is.   No, it isn't.
7. Is it cold in Los Angeles?   Yes, it is.   No, it isn't.
8. Is it cool in Vancouver?   Yes, it is.   No, it isn't.
9. Is it hot in Vancouver?   Yes, it is.   No, it isn't.
10. Is it warm in Hong Kong?   Yes, it is.   No, it isn't.

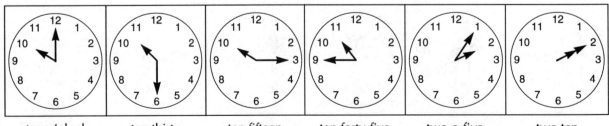

| ten o'clock | ten thirty | ten fifteen | ten forty-five | two-o-five | two ten |

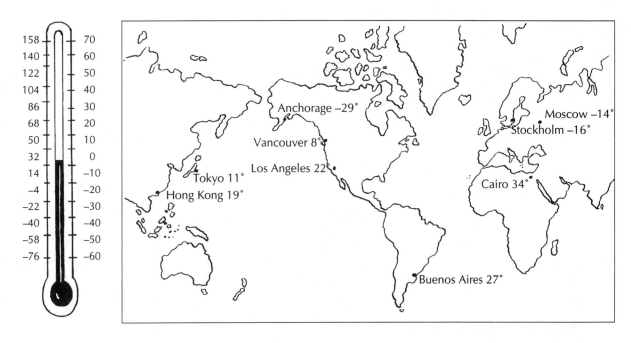

Listening and Speaking: Using Idioms

I've Got To Go Now

A. Practise the expressions with the teacher.

I have to leave.	= **I've got to go now.**
Enjoy your day.	= **Have a nice day.**
You have a nice day too.	= **You too.**

B. Listen and choose the answers.

1. It is 7:00.   Yes, it is.   No, it isn't.
2. Chen is late for work.   Yes, he is.   No, he isn't.

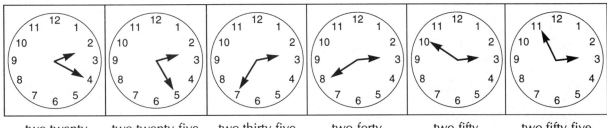

two twenty   two twenty-five   two thirty-five   two-forty   two-fifty   two fifty-five

C. Listen and write the words.

> **Chen:** What time is _____?
> **Lili:** It's 8 o'clock.
> **Chen:** Oh. I've _____ to go now. I'm late for work.
> **Lili:** Have a _____ day.
> **Chen:** You too.

D. Practise the conversation with a partner.

It's Freezing Today

A. Practise the expressions with the teacher.

Isn't it cold today?	= **Pretty cold weather, eh?**
It's very cold.	= **It's freezing.**
Yes.	= **Yeah.**

B. Listen and write the words.

> **Carla:** Hi. How _____ it going?
> **Tom:** Not bad.
> **Carla:** _____ cold weather, eh?
> **Tom:** It sure is. _____ freezing today.
> **Carla:** Yeah, winter is really cold in Canada.
> **Tom:** Well, see _____ later.
> **Carla:** 'Bye.

leave   freezing   work   seasons

C. Listen again and write the words.

Carla: Hi. _____'s it going?

Tom: _____ bad.

Carla: Pretty cold weather, eh?

Tom: It sure is. _____'s freezing today.

Carla: _____, winter is really cold in Canada.

Tom: Well, see you later.

Carla: 'Bye.

D. Practise the conversation with a partner.

Suggestions

Practise the conversations. Memorize one conversation. Act it out for the class.

Ten-Minute Grammar Games

Mystery Person

Focus: Review the verb **be**, practise giving personal information.

1. The teacher writes this information on the board:

   I am from . . .
   My job is . . .
   My language is . . .
   I am a . . . (man/woman).

2. Students copy and complete the information on a card or piece of paper.

3. Students put the cards in a box. The teacher reads a card. The students guess the name of the person who wrote the card.

Back and Forth

Focus: Practise questions and answers with the verb **be**.

The object of this game is to produce accurate questions and answers.

1. The teacher reviews question and short answer form with the class. The students practise a few questions and answers, and the teacher writes the questions and answers on the board.

2. Students work in pairs. They can take turns in front of the class, or work within a group of five or six. (If students speak in front of the class, they might need some practice time first.)

3. Student A asks Student B a question. Student B answers and then asks Student A a question, and so on:

   Student A: Are you 15 years old?

   Student B: No, I'm not. I'm 18 years old.

   Student B: Are you a doctor?

   Student A: No, I'm not. I'm a secretary.

4. Students continue in this way until someone makes a grammatical error. Other students in the class or group should point out the error, and help correct it.

5. When a student makes a mistake, he or she gets a point. Each pair should play the game for a few minutes. The student with the fewest points wins. Then a second set of students has a turn. Continue until everyone in the class has participated.

Test Yourself

Short Answers

Read and answer the questions. Use short answers.

A. Dino Conti is a pilot with International Airlines. He is Canadian. He is 34 years old. He is tall.

   Is Dino Conti a woman?   **No, he isn't.**

   1. Is Dino Conti a flight attendant?
   2. Is he from the United States?
   3. Is Dino Conti 30 years old?
   4. Is he tall?

B. Margaret and Diana are friends. They are from England. Margaret is a cook in a restaurant. Diana is an engineer. They are on vacation. They are in Spain. It is hot and sunny. They are happy.

   Are Margaret and Diana friends?   **Yes, they are.**

   1. Are Margaret and Diana from Spain?
   2. Is Diana a cook?
   3. Are they on vacation?
   4. Is the weather rainy?
   5. Are they happy in Spain?

Question Form

Write questions with the words.

   they / students / are / ?   **Are they students?**

   1. occupation / what / your / is / ?
   2. your / are / what / names / ?
   3. cold / is / San Diego / it / in / ?
   4. people / Chinese / in / are / Taiwan / ?
   5. rainy / is / Vancouver / in / it / ?

Negative Form

Seasons

Spring	**Summer**	**Fall (Autumn)**	**Winter**
March	June	September	December
April	July	October	January
May	August	November	February

Correct the information in the sentences.

July is in spring. **July isn't in spring. It's in summer.**

1. October and November are in summer.
2. April is in winter.
3. January is in spring.
4. July and August are in fall.
5. February is in summer.

Verb Review

A. Read the postcards. Write the missing verbs.

Is   are   is   Are   Is   it's

Dear Marcos,

How ____ you? How ____ the weather in Vancouver? ____ the summer hot or cold? In Caracas, ____ hot and sunny. ____ you happy there? ____ Pedro in your English class?

Write soon,

Maria

is   am   is   are   am   is   am

Dear Maria,

Thank you for your letter. I ____ fine. Pedro ____ fine too. We ____ in the same English class. He is very good at English. I ____ not good at English.

The weather here ____ not great, but today it is sunny and warm. I ____ happy in Vancouver. It ____ an interesting city.

See you soon,

Marcos

B. Answer the questions.

1. How is the weather in Caracas?
2. How is Marcos?
3. Are Pedro and Marcos in the same English class?
4. How is the weather in Vancouver?
5. Is Marcos happy in Vancouver?

Vocabulary

Choose the word that is different.

1. rainy, snowy, winter, sunny, cloudy
2. engineer, cook, teacher, doctor, class
3. English, Japanese, Canadian, China, Moroccan
4. January, Friday, Monday, Tuesday, Wednesday
5. fall, spring, hot, winter, summer

3

Demonstrative Adjectives "this," "that," "these," "those"

"Be" Simple Past Tense: Affirmative, Negative

Expressions of Past Time

Question Words "where," "when"

	Singular	Plural
Near	this	these
Far	that	those

Past Tense "Be" Affirmative

I was	we were
you were	you were
he was	they were
she was	
it was	

Negative

I was not	we were not
you were not	you were not
he was not	they were not
she was not	
it was not	

Contraction

I wasn't	we weren't
you weren't	you weren't
he wasn't	they weren't
she wasn't	
it wasn't	

Words You Need

Look at the pictures. Complete the chart on page 31.

A

B

C

	Picture A	Picture B	Picture C
1. a girl	✗		✗
2. a hotel		✗	
3. a mother			
4. a father			
5. a bank			
6. a bus			
7. a truck driver			
8. a boy			
9. a car			
10. a taxi			
11. a house			
12. a cat			
13. a store			
14. a tree			

a bank a bus a truck a car a taxi a house

Understanding Grammar

UNDERSTAND: Demonstrative Adjectives **this, that, these, those**

Use demonstrative adjectives to show a specific person or thing. There are four demonstrative adjectives.

	Singular	**Plural**
Near	this	these
Far	that	those

This book is small.
These books are big.

This man is Mr. Smith.
Those people are his children.

A. Choose the correct adjective.

1. (This/These) boy is my son.
2. (That/Those) children are happy.
3. (That/Those) tourists are tired.
4. (This/These) hotel is full.
5. (That/These) suitcase is small.

6. (That/Those) buildings are tall.
7. (This/These) people are hungry.
8. (This/These) city is big.
9. (That/Those) camera is expensive.
10. (That/Those) car is Japanese.

B. Which sentences are wrong? Correct wrong demonstrative adjectives.

1. This people are old.
2. Those suitcases are green.
3. That car is a Honda.
4. These truck is not big.
5. Those children are happy.

6. This tree is green.
7. These suitcase is small.
8. This hotel is new.
9. These people are teachers.
10. Those people are taxi drivers.

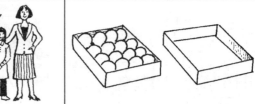

a tree   a store   a son   a daughter   full   empty

C. Look at the picture. Write the letter for the sentences:

That boy is happy.   **c**

1. That boy is happy.
2. This tree is green.
3. Those trees aren't green.
4. These people are tired.
5. This hotel is small.
6. This man is strong.
7. Those people are tourists.
8. This bus is new.
9. That dog is big.
10. This dog is small.

UNDERSTAND: "Be" Simple Past Tense

Use the simple past tense for situations that ended in past time. Use the forms **was** or **were**. Past time phrases (**yesterday, this morning, last week**) are sometimes used:

It **was** hot this morning.

They **were** late yesterday.

I was	we were
you were	you were
he was	they were
she was	
it was	

| young | old | busy | a hotel | afraid | a dog |

A. Which sentences are wrong? Correct wrong verbs.

1. The bus were late.
2. The people was happy.
3. The tour guide was Canadian.
4. The children was excited.
5. This street be busy.

6. The weather were rainy.
7. The police officer were a woman.
8. The cameras be expensive.
9. The tourists was lost.
10. Those women were tired.

B. Answer the questions.

at work   at home   at school

1. Where was Lili yesterday?
2. Where were Carla and Roberto yesterday?
3. Where was Tom yesterday?

C. This morning everyone was busy in the city. Where were these people?

a dentist   a post office   a movie   a drugstore   a restaurant   a hospital

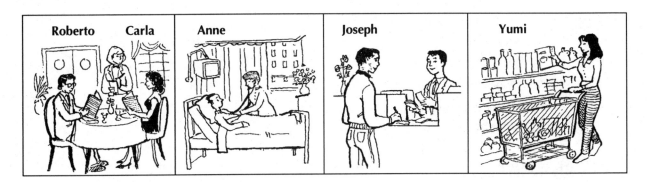

Work with a partner. Complete the chart.

People	Places
1. Anne	**at the hospital**
2. Lili and Chen	
3. Tom	
4. Nadia and her sister	
5. Roberto and Carla	
6. Yumi	
7. Max	
8. Joseph	

a sister   a brother   excited   a supermarket   expensive   cheap

UNDERSTAND: "Be" Simple Past Negative

Use **not** after the past form of the verb **be** for negative sentences:

She **was not** happy yesterday.

They **were not** late this morning.

Negative Full Form		Negative Contraction		Language in Transition
I was not	we were not	I wasn't	we weren't	The contraction is generally used for speaking and informal writing. The full form is for formal writing.
you were not	you were not	you weren't	you weren't	
he was not	they were not	he wasn't	they weren't	
she was not		she wasn't		
it was not		it wasn't		

A. Write negative sentences. Use contractions:

He was hungry. He **wasn't** hungry.

1. He was tired.
2. They were late.
3. It was cold yesterday.
4. I was wrong.
5. She was tall.

6. They were Japanese.
7. We were lost.
8. It was at two o'clock.
9. You were happy.
10. She was American.

B. Change verbs to the correct form.

Yesterday I **was** not happy. Everything were wrong. The hotel was busy. People was not on time. The tour bus be late. It was not big. We was not comfortable. The tour guide was not polite. The weather be bad. People was not happy.

C. Talk about your class yesterday. Answer the questions with short answers.

1. Were you in class?   Yes, I was.   No, I wasn't.
2. Were you early?   Yes, I was.   No, I wasn't.
3. Was the teacher late?   Yes, he/she was.   No, he/she wasn't.
4. Was the class hard?   Yes, it was.   No, it wasn't.

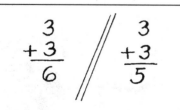

right   wrong   lost   comfortable   tour guide   polite

5. Were the students tired?	Yes, they were.	No, they weren't.
6. Was the weather hot?	Yes, it was.	No it wasn't.
7. Was your partner happy?	Yes, he/she was.	No, he/she wasn't.
8. Was the homework easy?	Yes, it was.	No, it wasn't.
9. Were you hungry?	Yes, I was.	No, I wasn't.
10. Were the windows big?	Yes, they were.	No, they weren't

UNDERSTAND: **Expressions of Past Time**

Use adverbs to show past time. Adverbs of time are:

> one word: **yesterday**

or   a phrase: **on Friday, last night, this morning.**

> Adverbs of past time answer the question **when.**

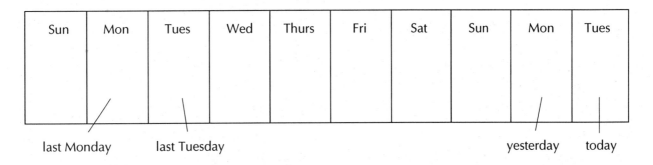

Sun	Mon	Tues	Wed	Thurs	Fri	Sat	Sun	Mon	Tues

last Monday   last Tuesday   yesterday   today

Look at Ali's calendar on page 38. Answer the questions.

> When was Ali at the book store?   **last Tuesday**

1. When was Ali at the bank?
2. When was he at the dentist?
3. When was he at the garage?
4. When was he at the airport?
5. What day were he and Nadia at the restaurant?
6. When was he at home watching TV?
7. What day were he and Nadia at the movies?
8. When was he at a party?

easy   hard   a party   TV/television   a garage   at home

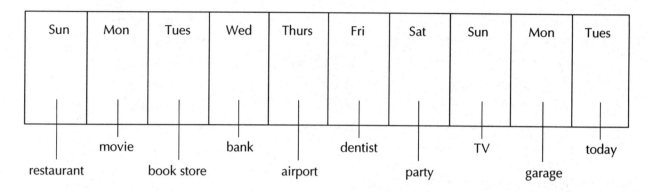

Sun	Mon	Tues	Wed	Thurs	Fri	Sat	Sun	Mon	Tues

restaurant   movie   book store   bank   airport   dentist   party   TV   garage   today

Listening and Speaking: Using Idioms

What a Nice Family!

A. Practise the expressions with the teacher.

photograph (photo)	= **picture**
children	= **kids**
That is a nice family!	= **What a nice family!**

B. Listen and answer the questions.

1. Lili's husband is on the left.   Yes, he is.   No, he isn't.
2. Lili's son is three years old.   Yes, he is.   No, he isn't.
3. Lili's daughter is three years old.   Yes, she is.   No, she isn't.

C. Listen and write the words.

Anne: Is this a picture _____ your family, Lili?

Lili: Yes, it is. That's my husband on the left.

Anne: Are those your _____?

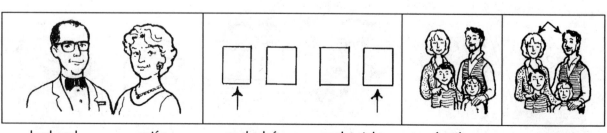

husband   wife   on the left   on the right   family   parents

Lili: Yes, they are.

Anne: How _____ are they?

Lili: My son is five and my daughter is three.

Anne: What _____ nice family!

D. Practise the conversation with a partner.

Hurry Up, We're Late!

A. Practise the expressions with the teacher.

Go fast!	= **Hurry up!**
there	= **over there**
here	= **right here**
It is time to go.	= **Let's go.**

B. Listen and write the words.

Nadia: Hurry _____, Ali. We're late.

Ali: Where is my camera?

Nadia: It's _____ there.

Ali: Where are my keys?

Nadia: They're _____ here.

Ali: Okay. Let_____ go.

C. Practise the conversation with a partner.

Suggestions

Practise the conversation "Hurry Up, We're Late!" Memorize it. Act it out for the class.

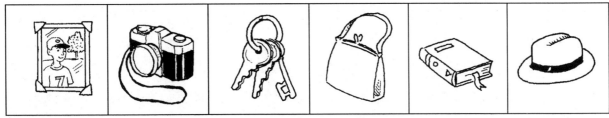

a photo   a camera   keys   a purse   a book   a hat

Ten-Minute Grammar Games

The Question Game

Focus: Practise questions and answers using **be** and the simple past tense. Practise with prepositions of location.

1. On a piece of paper, each student writes a date and a place where he or she was on that date.

2. Students work in groups of three or four. Student A tells the group the date on the piece of paper. Other students in the group take turns asking questions to find out where Student A was on that date. Student A answers only, "Yes I was" or "No, I wasn't":

Were you at the supermarket?	No, I wasn't.
Were you at home?	No, I wasn't.
Were you at the movies?	Yes, I was!

    When someone guesses correctly, Student A must show the piece of paper. If no one guesses within ten questions, Student A shows the piece of paper.

3. The first person to guess where Student A was, is the winner. Then he or she takes a turn answering questions. If no one guesses, Student A chooses another student to take a turn.

Chain

Focus: Practise pronouns and the simple past tense with **be**. This game can be played with the whole class or with smaller groups if the class is large.

1. The teacher begins with a statement such as, "Yesterday I was at the movies."

2. The first student repeats and then adds on. The second student repeats what was said by the teacher and the first student, and then adds on:

    Teacher: Yesterday I was at the movies.

    Student A: Yesterday she was at the movies. I was at the supermarket.

    Student B: Yesterday, she was at the movies. He was at the supermarket. I was at the airport.

3. Students continue until someone breaks the chain by forgetting, or by making a grammatical error.

4. Someone begins a new chain.

The teacher keeps track of how long the class can sustain the chain. This game can be repeated at another time, either to review structures or to practise new structures. Each time, students try to beat their previous class record.

Find Someone

Focus: Reviews questions and answers with the past tense of the verb **be**.

1. To help students remember question and answer forms, the teacher writes on the board:

    Were you . . . ? Yes, I was. No, I wasn't.

2. The aim is for students to find people who did the activities on the list below. Students walk around the room asking each other questions. When a student answers "Yes," his or her name is written beside the item. The first person to finish is the winner.

Find someone who:

1. was at home last night
2. was in a restaurant last weekend
3. was in class last Thursday
4. was in a bank yesterday
5. was in a supermarket yesterday afternoon
6. was in a store last Saturday

7. was at a party last weekend
8. was at the movies last night
9. was at the dentist last month
10. was in the library yesterday
11. was at home yesterday morning
12. was in a drugstore last week

Test Yourself

Demonstrative Adjectives

Write **This**, **That**, **These**, or **Those**

1. _____ children are happy.
2. _____ hotel is big.
3. _____ dog is friendly.

4. _____ flowers are beautiful.
5. _____ trees are green.

Verbs ("was," "were," "wasn't," "weren't")

A. Write **was** or **were**.

1. Yesterday the weather _____ sunny.
2. Where _____ you last night?
3. Last January I _____ in Mexico.
4. You _____ hungry this morning.
5. Yesterday _____ a holiday.
6. At eleven o'clock Max _____ in bed.

7. Carla and Roberto _____ at a party last weekend.
8. The hotel _____ small.
9. The tourists _____ tired after the trip.
10. Yumi _____ nervous in New York.

B. Read the story. Answer the questions.

Yumi was in New York last weekend. She was happy, but she was nervous. It was her first visit to New York. Yumi was in New York with her friend Anne. Anne wasn't nervous. This wasn't her first visit to New York. She was a good guide for Yumi. The two friends were very busy. They were in restaurants, in department stores, and at theatres. On Monday they were tired.

1. Where were Yumi and Anne last weekend?
2. Was Yumi nervous?
3. Was Anne nervous?
4. Was Yumi a guide?
5. Where were they in New York?
6. When were they tired?

Ask Questions

Ali was at home at three o'clock. (tired) **Was he tired?**

1. My friends were in London last week. (weather/good)
2. Roberto was at a movie last night. (good)
3. Chen and Lili were at the restaurant. (hungry)
4. The tourists were in the hotel restaurant. (food/good)
5. The hotel was big. (new)

Vocabulary

Write the letters.

1. a__rport
2. h__ngry
3. happ__
4. bu__lding
5. p__cture
6. ch__ld
7. su__tcase
8. we__ther
9. resta__rant
10. mov__es
11. y__ung
12. str__ng
13. t__red
14. h__tel
15. brot__er
16. yeste__day
17. c__mera
18. b__s
19. mo__her
20. g__od

4

"Can" to Express Ability
Indefinite Articles "a," "an"
Possessive Adjectives "my," "his," "her," "its," "our," "your," "their"

"Can" Affirmative		Negative Full Form		Negative Contraction		Question	
I can		I cannot		I can't		can I	
you can		you cannot		you can't		can you	
he can		he cannot		he can't		can he	
she can	go	she cannot	go	she can't	go	can she	go?
it can		it cannot		it can't		can it	
we can		we cannot		we can't		can we	
you can		you cannot		you can't		can you	
they can		they cannot		they can't		can they	

Words You Need

Look at the pictures. Match the pictures to the words.

1. play the guitar
2. speak Spanish
3. cook rice
4. drive a car
5. eat with chopsticks
6. play tennis

7. cook eggs
8. play soccer
9. eat with a fork
10. use a washing machine
11. use a camera
12. play the piano

Understanding Grammar

UNDERSTAND: **"Can" to Express Ability**

Use **can** before a main verb to show ability:

> He **can** speak English.
>
> I **can** play the guitar.

After **can** use the base form of the verb (no ending):

> Wrong: ✗ She can plays the guitar.
>
> Right: ✔ She can play the guitar.

Affirmative	
I can	
you can	
he can	
she can	play the guitar
it can	
we can	
you can	
they can	

A. Put the auxiliary verb **can** in the sentences. Correct the main verb.

1. Yumi plays the piano.
2. Carla cooks rice.
3. Joseph drives a car.
4. Lili uses a camera.
5. Tom and Max play tennis.
6. Chen plays the piano.
7. Anne uses a washing machine.
8. Nadia speaks Arabic and Spanish.
9. Max drives to school.
10. Chen and Lili eat with chopsticks.

> **TEACHER'S BOX:** Students may fail to use the base form after the modal auxiliary **can**. If they are familiar with the rule for the third person **s**, they may produce sentences such as "She cans read" or "She can reads."

B. Match the actions on the left with the things on the right:

You can write   with a pencil.

1.	You can drink coffee	with a pencil.
2.	You can take photographs	from a book.
3.	You can write letters	with a camera.
4.	You can drive to work	with chopsticks.
5.	You can play music	in a car.
6.	You can read	on a telephone.
7.	You can eat Chinese food	with a guitar.
8.	You can speak to people	from a cup.

to play guitar   to cook   to drive   to eat   to play tennis   to use chopsticks

UNDERSTAND: **"Can" Negative**

Add **not** to **can** = **cannot**:

I **cannot** speak English.
I **can't** speak English.

Negative Full Form	
I cannot you cannot he cannot she cannot it cannot we cannot you cannot they cannot	speak Russian

Negative Contraction	
I can't you can't he can't she can't it can't we can't you can't they can't	speak Greek

A. Write negative sentences. Use the full form **cannot.**

1. I can speak Japanese.
2. He can drive a bus.
3. She can write.
4. They can read French.
5. We can cook spaghetti.
6. You can play piano.
7. I can carry that suitcase.
8. We can eat with a fork.
9. He can use a washing machine.
10. She can use a computer.

B. Write negative sentences. Use the contraction.

1. Lili can use a camera.
2. Max can drive a truck.
3. They can read Spanish.
4. She can play soccer.
5. It can walk.
6. Joseph can cook eggs.
7. Roberto can speak two languages.
8. Yumi can play tennis.
9. You can read Hungarian.
10. They can understand me.

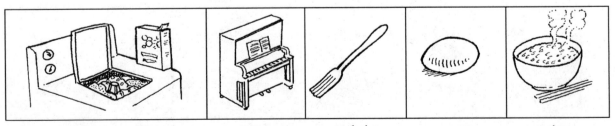

a washing machine   a piano   a fork   an egg   rice

UNDERSTAND: **"Can" Question Form**

Use **can** before the subject to form a question. Use the base form of the main verb after **can**:

Can you speak English?

Affirmative	
I can	
you can	
he can	
she can	go
it can	
we can	
you can	
they can	

Question	
can I	
can you	
can he	
can she	go?
can it	
can we	
can you	
can they	

> **TEACHER'S BOX:** The interrogative form of **can** is used to ask about ability. It is often used to ask for permission as well. The examples below are about ability.

A. Match the question and the picture.

1. Can she walk?
2. Can you help me?
3. Can it talk?
4. Can he use a computer?
5. Can they understand me?
6. Can we carry it?

spaghetti	a cup	a computer
a letter	a telephone	to play soccer

B. Work with a partner. Ask questions. Talk about you. Give one answer:

Can you play the guitar? **Yes, I can** or **No, I can't.**

1. play tennis
2. speak two languages
3. cook rice
4. use a computer
5. drive a car

6. play soccer
7. use a camera
8. speak Japanese
9. eat with chopsticks
10. drive a truck

UNDERSTAND: **Indefinite Articles**

Singular Noun	Before a Consonant	Before a Vowel
a/an	**a** doctor	**an** orderly
Plural Noun	Before a Consonant	Before a Vowel
Ø	doctors	orderlies

wrong: ✗ I have apple.

right: ✔ have an apple.

TEACHER'S BOX: Some students confuse **one** with **a**. In English, **one** refers to the specific number of things being counted, e.g., **one** apple, not three. **A** refers to one example of a category.

to understand   to carry   to talk   to walk   to help   an orderly

A. Look at the jobs. Write **a** or **an**:

an actor, **a** bus driver

___ teacher   ___ engineer   ___ mechanic   ___ librarian   ___ teller

___ orderly   ___ clerk   ___ cashier   ___ artist   ___ doctor

B. Look at the pictures in Exercise A. Write the jobs.

1. She works in a school. What is she?   **a teacher**
2. He works in an engineering office. What is he?
3. He works in a garage. What is he?
4. He works in a library. What is he?
5. She works in a bank. What is she?
6. He works in a hospital. What is he?
7. He works in a store. What is he?
8. She works in a supermarket. What is she?
9. He works in a studio. What is he?
10. She works in a hospital. What is she?

a chair   an apple   an office   a studio   an artist   a cashier

UNDERSTAND: **Possessive Adjectives**

Possessive adjectives show **who** owns something. Use possessive adjectives before nouns:

not "**a** cat" (general), but "**my** cat" (possession)

a cat

my cat

Subject Pronouns	Possessive Adjectives
I	my
you	your
he	his
she	her
it	its
we	our
you	your
they	their

TEACHER'S BOX: Possessive adjectives are confusing to students for two reasons:
1. They refer to the possessor, not to the object possessed. (English nouns are not marked for gender.)
2. They are irregular in their formation and have to be learned by rote.

A. Complete the sentences with a possessive adjective.

my   your   his   her   our   their

Yumi is a teacher. These are **her** students.

1. We are in class. This is _____ class.
2. Joseph drives a car. That is _____ car.
3. I work in this office. _____ office is big.
4. Rita is Canadian. Canada is _____ country.
5. Ali and Nadia are Egyptian. Egypt is _____ country.
6. They work in a bank. _____ bank is old.
7. Lili uses that cup. It is _____ cup.
8. What are _____ names?
9. Max is a mechanic. He likes _____ job.
10. Hi Eric. Is that _____ car?

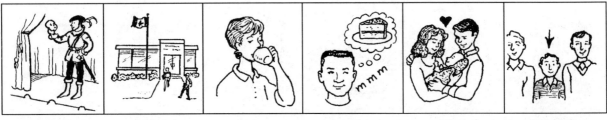

an actor   a school   to use a cup   to like   to love   between

B. Put the possessive adjectives in the paragraph. Use each word once.

his   their   his   his   her

This is the Sanchez family. They are near _____ house. Tony Sanchez is between _____ son and _____ daughter. Susanna is near _____ father. Tomas is near _____ mother.

Lea Sanchez   Tomas Sanchez   Tony Sanchez   Susanna Sanchez

C. Put the possessive adjectives in the letter. Use each word once.

my   our   her   his   your

Dear Lili,

This is my family. We are near _____ house in Mexico. That is _____ husband Roberto. Pedro is near _____ father. Maria is near _____ brother. Please send a picture of _____ family.

Your friend,

Carla

a sister   a brother   a husband   a wife   a grandmother   a grandfather

Listening and Speaking: Using Idioms

Can I Leave My Number?

A. Practise the expressions with the teacher.

I am sorry.	= **Sorry.**
Thank you.	= **Thanks.**
Goodbye.	= **'Bye.**

B. Listen and answer the questions.

1. Max:
   a) is at home
   b) isn't at home

2. Yumi wants to:
   a) leave her number
   b) leave her name

3. The number is:
   a) 331-2878
   b) 732-2878
   c) 731-2878

C. Listen and write the words.

Yumi: Hello. Can I speak _____ Max please?

Father: _____ , he isn't home.

Yumi: This is Yumi. Can I leave my number?

Father: Sure. What _____ the number?

Yumi: It's 731-2878.

Father: Can you repeat _____?

Yumi: Sure. It's 731-2878.

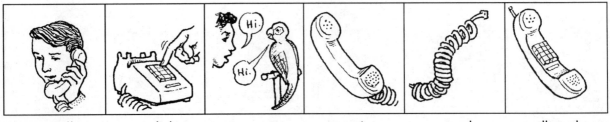

to call   to dial   to repeat   a receiver   a cord   a cordless phone

D. Practise the conversation with a partner.

Sorry, Wrong Number

A. Practise the expressions with the teacher.

The telephone number is wrong.	= **You have the wrong number.**
I'm sorry. I made a mistake.	= **Excuse me.**
It is okay.	= **No problem.**

B. Listen and write the words.

Carla: Hello. Anne?

Woman: Anne?

Carla: Yes, can I speak to Anne please?

Woman: _____ sorry. You have the wrong number.

Carla: Is _____ 326-1769?

Woman: No, it isn't.

Carla: Excuse me.

Woman: That's okay. _____ no problem.

C. Practise the conversation with a partner.

Suggestions

Memorize a telephone conversation. Act it out for the class.

| a telephone book | the yellow pages | a pay phone | buttons | to write |

Ten-Minute Grammar Games

I Spy

Focus: Practise possessive adjectives. Review demonstrative adjectives.

1. Each student takes out three or four objects (e.g., a pencil, a stapler, an eraser). The teacher divides the objects into two groups, and puts half the objects on one side of the room and half on the other.

2. The teacher calls the name of each student, one at a time. The student, depending on his or her position in the room, says "That's my book. These are my pencils," etc. When the student says the sentence correctly, he or she can retrieve the object.

Mystery Person

Focus: Review the verb **can** to express ability.

1. On a piece of paper, each student writes five things he or she can or can't do:

   I can ski. I can play the guitar. I can speak French. I can't speak Spanish. I can't drive a car.

2. The students put the papers in a box. The teacher picks a paper and reads the list. Students guess which person has written this list.

Option: Students can take turns picking papers from the box and reading them to the class.

Find Someone

Focus: Practise questions and answers with **can** to express ability. Practise some common verbs.

The teacher writes these phrases on the board to help the students:

   Can you . . . ? Yes, I can. No, I can't.

The aim is for students to find people who can do the activities on the list below. Students walk around the room asking each other questions about what they can and can't do. When a student answers "Yes," his or her name is written beside the activity. The first person to finish is the winner.

Find someone who can:

1. play the piano
2. read Japanese
3. speak Spanish
4. swim
5. drive a car
6. eat with chopsticks
7. cook eggs
8. write in Italian
9. speak three languages
10. use a computer
11. cook rice
12. play the guitar

Test Yourself

Verbs

A. Write **can** or **can't**.

1. Max is a mechanic. He _____ fix cars.
2. Tom is a flight attendant. He _____ fly planes.
3. Marianne is an English teacher. She _____ teach grammar.
4. Anne is a doctor. She _____ help sick people.
5. Alex is five years old. He _____ drive a car.

B. Write questions with **can**:

piano / Roberto / play/ ? **Can Roberto play piano?**

1. tennis / play / Joseph / ?
2. French / you / speak / ?
3. a car / Nadia / drive ?
4. Max / good pictures / take / ?
5. spaghetti / cook / Yumi / ?

Possessive Adjectives

Complete the sentences. Use **my, his, her, our, your, their**.

1. I am very cold. _____ hands are freezing.
2. Jenny and Joe are grandparents. _____ grandson is three years old.
3. We aren't tired. _____ vacation was great.
4. Max is strong. _____ suitcase is heavy.
5. Hello Roberto. Is this _____ daughter?
6. Yumi is happy. _____ weekend was interesting.

Indefinite Articles

Use **a** or **an**.

1. _____ engineer
2. _____ piano
3. _____ camera
4. _____ suitcase
5. _____ apple
6. _____ child
7. _____ fork
8. _____ guitar
9. _____ animal
10. _____ orderly

Conversations

Complete the conversations.

1. **Anne:** _____ I please speak to Nadia?
   Ali: She _____ come to the phone right now. _____ I take a message?

2. **Student:** This exercise is very hard.
   Teacher: _____ I help you?
   Student: Yes. _____ you help me with the new words?

3. **Lili:** The party is at seven on Saturday.
   Yumi: _____ I cook some food?
   Lili: Sure, you _____ make a salad.

Vocabulary

Match the job and the place.

1. an orderly	a) a theatre
2. a teacher	b) a bus
3. a mechanic	c) a supermarket
4. a teller	d) an airplane
5. a police officer	e) a hospital
6. an actor	f) a library
7. a librarian	g) a school
8. a cashier	h) a garage
9. a flight attendant	i) a bank
10. a bus driver	j) a police car

5 Review Unit

At the Hotel

A. Read about the tourists. Fill in the hotel registration cards.

Anne Martin is a doctor. She is Canadian. She comes from Montreal. She is 26 years old. Her language is French but she can speak English.

Joseph Muna is from Cameroon. He is an accountant. He is 25 years old. He speaks three languages, English, French, and Ewondo.

Mr. and Mrs. Lopez are Mexican. His name is Roberto. He is 29 years old. Her name is Carla. She is 27 years old. Their language is Spanish, but they can speak English. He is an orderly. She is a secretary.

Max is a young man from Russia. His family name is Kuslov. He is 19 years old. He was a student in Russia but he is a mechanic today. He can speak Russian and English, but he can't speak Spanish.

58

Mr. and Mrs. Han are from Hong Kong. Their first names are Chen and Lili. Lili is 25 years old. Her husband is 31. He is a photographer and she is a bank teller. They speak Cantonese and English.

Yumi Suzuki is from Japan. She is 24 years old. She isn't from Tokyo. Her city is Kyoto. Yumi is a teacher. She can speak Japanese and English.

Nadia and Ali Aziz are from Egypt. She is an engineer and he is a bank manager. They are 34 and 38 years old. They can speak Arabic and English.

Tom Kirk is 28 years old. He is American. He is from Los Angeles. Tom was a police officer. He wasn't happy. Now he is a flight attendant and he can fly to different cities. He can speak English and Japanese.

female = a woman   **male** = a man

Example:

Family name:	**Martin**
First name:	**Anne**
Age:	**26**
Sex:	**female**
Country:	**Canada**
Languages:	**English, French**
Occupation:	**doctor**

Family name:	Muna
First name:	
Age:	
Sex:	
Country:	Cameroon
Languages:	
Occupation:	

Family name:	Lopez
First name:	
Age:	29
Sex:	
Country:	
Languages:	
Occupation:	

Family name:	
First name:	Max
Age:	
Sex:	
Country:	
Languages:	
Occupation:	mechanic

Family name:	
First name:	Lili
Age:	
Sex:	female
Country:	
Languages:	
Occupation:	

Family name:	
First name:	
Age:	24
Sex:	
Country:	
Languages:	Japanese, English
Occupation	

Family name:	
First name:	Nadia
Age:	
Sex:	female
Country:	
Languages:	
Occupation:	

Family name:	
First name:	
Age:	28
Sex:	
Country:	United States
Languages:	
Occupation:	

B. Answer the questions.

1. What languages can Anne speak?
2. How old is Mrs. Lopez?
3. What is Joseph's job?
4. What languages can Max speak?
5. Is Chen a woman?
6. How old is Lili Han?
7. What city is Yumi from?
8. What nationality are Nadia and Ali?
9. How old is Nadia?
10. Where is Tom Kirk from?

Country and Nationality

A. Match countries to nationalities.

1. France	Chinese
2. China	Brazilian
3. Spain	Turkish
4. Canada	Vietnamese
5. Viet Nam	Canadian
6. United States	Indonesian
7. Turkey	French
8. Indonesia	Australian
9. Brazil	American
10. Australia	Spanish

60

B. Work with two partners. Answer the questions.

1. What is your country?
2. What is your nationality?
3. Where are your partners from?
4. What are the nationalities of your partners?
5. What languages can your partners speak?

Conversations

Check In

Read the conversation. Write the words.

Clerk: Good morning. _____ I help you?

Roberto: Yes. We _____ with the tour group.

Clerk: What is your family name?

Roberto: _____ name is Lopez. I'm Roberto. _____ wife's name is Carla.

Clerk: _____ are you from Mr. Lopez?

Roberto: We're from Mexico.

Clerk: Welcome to the hotel.

New Friends

Read the conversation. Write the words.

Anne: Hello. _____ name is Anne Martin.

Nadia: Hello, Anne. _____ to meet you. I'm Nadia Aziz. This _____ my husband Ali.

Anne: I'm pleased to _____ you. Where are you from Nadia?

Nadia: We're from Cairo. _____ are you from Anne?

Anne: I'm from Montreal. _____ 's in Canada.

Families

A. Match names for male and female people in the family:

mother   father

Female	Male
1. sister	husband
2. aunt	brother
3. grandmother	father
4. wife	son
5. mother	uncle
6. granddaughter	grandfather
7. daughter	grandson

B. Write **was** or **were**.

Last Saturday afternoon was fun. The weather _____ hot and sunny. My family and I _____ in a new city. We _____ tourists. My father _____ the driver. My sister _____ the tour guide. My brother _____ the photographer. The afternoon _____ fun. We _____ happy.

Postcards from Banff

Read the postcards on this page and on page 62. Answer the questions:

Where are the postcards from?   **They are from Banff.**

1. Can Yumi and Anne speak English?
2. How old is Anne?
3. What can Ali do in good weather?
4. Why are Nadia and Ali happy at the hotel?
5. What can Ali and Nadia do after dinner?
6. When weren't Lili and Chen happy?
7. When was the weather cold and snowy?
8. Where is Max?
9. What is the server's name?
10. What can the tennis coach speak?

Dear Keiko,

This is a good vacation. I can speak English with my new friend Anne. She is from Montreal. She is a doctor. She is 26 years old. We are good friends.

Yumi

Greetings from Banff!

Nadia and I are happy in this hotel.
It is beautiful. We can play tennis
or swim at the hotel in good weather.
After dinner we can listen to music.
It is fun at the hotel.

Ali

Hello from Banff!

On the weekend we weren't happy.
It was cold and rainy. This week it
is hot and sunny. Last winter, it was
snowy and the weather was cold. I
am happy we weren't here last
winter.

Lili

Dear Grandma,

I am in a big, old hotel. You can see
different people here.

The server is short and fat. He has
a long moustache. His name is Joe.
The tennis coach is tall and strong.
He has black hair. He can speak
three languages. My vacation is fun.

Love, Max

6

Verb "Have"
"Any" in Negatives and Questions
Possessive Nouns
Spelling Plural Nouns Ending in "y"

"Have" Affirmative

I have
you have
he has
she has   a cat
it has

we have
you have
they have

Negative

I do not have
you do not have
he does not have
she does not have   a cat
it does not have

we do not have
you do not have
they do not have

Contraction

I don't have
you don't have
he doesn't have
she doesn't have   a cat
it doesn't have

we don't have
you don't have
they don't have

Question

do I have
do you have
does he have
does she have   a cat?
does it have

do we have
do you have
do they have

Words You Need

Work with a partner. Look at the pictures. Complete the chart.

Apartment A

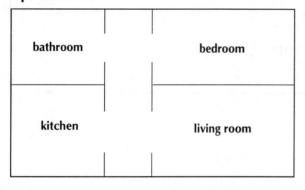

Apartment B

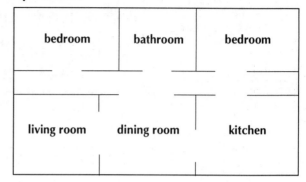

Apartment C

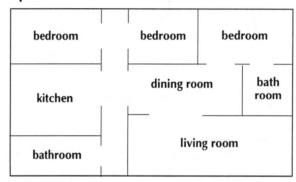

	Apartment A	Apartment B	Apartment C
1. four rooms	✗		
2. three bedrooms			
3. eight rooms			
4. one bathroom			
5. a living room and a dining room			
6. no dining room			
7. two bedrooms			
8. one bedroom			
9. a kitchen			
10. two bathrooms			

Understanding Grammar

UNDERSTAND: **Verb "Have"**

"Have" Affirmative	
I have you have **he has** **she has** **it has** we have you have they have	a cat

TEACHER'S BOX **Have** is used as a stative verb to show possession. (He **has** blond hair. He **has** a car.) The dynamic use of **have**, which is more difficult for some students, is not looked at here.

Use the verb **have** with:

Possession:
We have a dog.
That house has small windows.

The Weather:
Canada has cold winters.
Singapore has hot weather.

Description:
She has short hair.
He has a moustache.

Appointments:
I have a class at five.
He has a doctor's appointment on Friday.

 Friday
May 6 ✗ Dr. Finch

Sickness:
She has a headache.
He has a cold.

a living room   a dining room   a bathroom   a bedroom   a kitchen

A. Which sentences are wrong? Correct errors in the verbs.

1. Yumi has a big suitcase.
2. Roberto and Carla have two children.
3. Tom has a big apartment.
4. You has a brother.
5. Toronto has cold winters.
6. He have a car and a bicycle.
7. We has a cat.
8. The house has five rooms.
9. You has three children.
10. She have new glasses.

> **TEACHER'S BOX** In English, adjectives go before the noun and are always singular. They do not agree with plural nouns:
>
> wrong ✗ their camera expensive
> wrong ✗ their expensives cameras
> right ✔ their expensive camera
> right ✔ their expensive cameras

B. Use the correct form of **have**.

1. We _____ an appointment at the dentist.
2. My parents _____ a new car.
3. Max _____ an apartment in my building.
4. I _____ a cold.
5. My friend _____ a moustache.
6. She _____ long hair.
7. New York _____ hot summers.
8. The children _____ a dog and a cat.
9. Those people _____ a piano.
10. They _____ a tree near their house.

C. Work with a partner. Look at the picture on page 67. Write the name of the person or people for each sentence:

A young woman has two children. **Susan**

1. A young woman has two children.
2. A short man has a moustache.
3. A young girl has long hair.
4. An old woman has glasses.
5. A young man has a suitcase.
6. Two children have a dog.
7. A young woman has a guitar.
8. A man and woman have a baby.
9. An old man has a newspaper.
10. Two people have cameras.

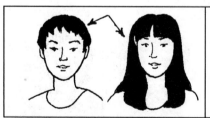
short hair   long hair

a moustache

a beard   a bicycle

glasses

UNDERSTAND: **"Have" Negative**

Use **do not** + base form of **have** for negation. Use **does not** with "he," "she," and "it":

I **do not** have a car.

She **does not** have a car.

Negative

I do not have you do not have	
he does not have she does not have it does not have	a cat
we do not have you do not have they do not have	

a newspaper   a baby   a cold   a headache   a backache   an earache

UNDERSTAND: **"Have" Negative Contraction**

Use **don't** = do not. Use **doesn't** = does not:

> He **doesn't** have a car.
> We **don't** have a car.

Negative Contraction

I don't have
you don't have
he doesn't have
she doesn't have   a cat
it doesn't have

we don't have
you don't have
they don't have

Language in Transition

It is common to use the contraction in speaking and informal writing.

A.   Write negative sentences. Use contractions:

I have a sister.   **I don't have a sister.**

1. Max has a moustache.
2. He has a wife.
3. Carla has long hair.
4. Lili and Chen have a daughter.
5. Nadia has blue eyes.

6. Anne has a dog.
7. Yumi has a big family.
8. They have a big apartment.
9. We have short hair.
10. Tom has an old car.

B.   Which sentences are wrong? Correct errors in the verbs.

1. She doesn't has a big apartment.
2. They don't have a new house.
3. Joseph don't have a brother.
4. Yumi and Lili doesn't have cameras.
5. Tony doesn't have a moustache.

6. I don't have a bicycle.
7. We doesn't have a car.
8. Nadia doesn't has an umbrella.
9. They don't have a sister.
10. She don't have a piano.

a toothache

a sprained ankle

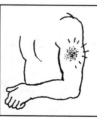
a cut

a bruise

a fever

a broken bone

UNDERSTAND: **Using "Any" in Negative Sentences**

When the number of objects is indefinite, use **some** or **any** before the noun. Use **some** in affirmative sentences. Use **any** in negative sentences with **plural** nouns:

I have **some** books.   Wrong ✗ I don't have some books.

I don't have **any** books.   Wrong ✗ I don't have any book.

A. Write the sentences in the negative:

I have **some** paper.   I **don't** have **any** paper.

1. We have some friends in Italy.
2. Max has some pictures of his family.
3. Lili has some cousins in China.
4. That school has some English classes.
5. Montreal has some hot days in winter.
6. Yumi has some apples.
7. I have some relatives in Los Angeles.
8. Our new apartment has some big windows.
9. Anne has some sisters.
10. Our class has some students from Korea.

B. Write **some** or **any**.

1. We have _____ cousins in Australia.
2. Tom doesn't have _____ young children.
3. Lili has _____ friends in Kyoto.
4. That college has _____ students from Iran.
5. We don't have _____ books about travel.
6. Anne and Yumi don't have _____ suitcases.
7. Nadia doesn't have _____ brothers in Canada.
8. That store has _____ books about tennis.
9. They have _____ grammar books.
10. I don't have _____ pencils.

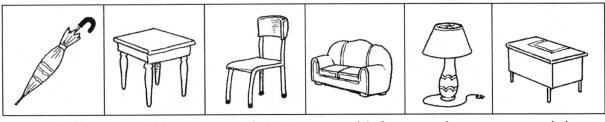

an umbrella   a table   a chair   a couch/sofa   a lamp   a desk

UNDERSTAND: **"Have" Question Form**

Put **do** before the subject and verb. Use **does** with "he," "she," and "it." Put a question mark (**?**) at the end of the sentence:

They have a sister.   **Do they have a sister?**

He has a moustache.   **Does he have a moustache?**

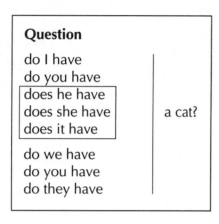

Question

do I have
do you have
does he have
does she have   a cat?
does it have

do we have
do you have
do they have

TEACHER'S BOX The form "**Do you have +** **noun?**" is used to ask questions about possessions. British English sometimes substitutes the form "**Have you +** noun?"

A.   Write questions:

You have two sisters.   **Do you have two sisters?**

1.   He has a new bicycle.
2.   We have a good teacher.
3.   She has a friend in Texas.
4.   They have a new house.
5.   Roberto has a new car.

6.   His brother has a moustache.
7.   They have a child.
8.   Anne has short hair.
9.   Nadia and Lili have long hair.
10.   Kyoto has a good climate.

B.   Read and choose the answers.

Max has a big apartment. His apartment has six rooms: a living room, a kitchen, a dining room, a bathroom, and two bedrooms. The apartment is in a big building. Max has two friends in the building, John and Bob. John has a small apartment. His apartment has three rooms: a bedroom, a kitchen, and a bathroom. Bob's apartment isn't small, but it isn't big. It has four rooms: a living room, a kitchen, a bedroom, and a bathroom.

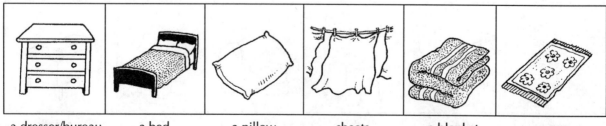

a dresser/bureau   a bed   a pillow   sheets   a blanket   a rug

1. Does Max have a big apartment?	Yes, he does.	No, he doesn't.
2. Does his apartment have six rooms?	Yes, it does.	No, it doesn't.
3. Does Max have friends in the building?	Yes, he does.	No, he doesn't.
4. Does John have a big apartment?	Yes, he does.	No, he doesn't.
5. Does John's apartment have three rooms?	Yes, it does.	No, it doesn't.
6. Do John and Bob's apartments have kitchens?	Yes, they do.	No, they don't.
7. Do all the apartments have living rooms?	Yes, they do.	No, they don't.

> **TEACHER'S BOX** The alternative short answer form is, "Yes, they have", "Yes, she has" or "No, they haven't", "No, he hasn't." This alternative is more common in British English.

UNDERSTAND: **Spelling Plural Nouns Ending in "y"**

Nouns Ending in **y**			
Vowel + **y**	add **s**	day key	days keys
Consonant + **y**	change **y** to **i**, add **es**	city activity	cities activities

A. Write the plurals.

1. Yumi and Anne are _____. (friend)
2. New York and Tokyo are big _____. (city)
3. My two _____ are Rick and Sam. (brother)
4. Ali and Nadia have three _____. (child)
5. These _____ are late for class. (student)
6. Those _____ are my friends. (woman)
7. Canada and the United States are big _____. (country)
8. I am in class three _____ a week. (day)
9. Carla has five _____. (cousin)
10. The students have _____ on Friday and Saturday nights. (party)
11. We have big _____. (family)
12. My _____ are on the table. (key)

| a bookcase | a drawer | a mirror | a picture | a cushion | a garden |

B. Write the plural of these words. Put them in the crossword puzzle.

Across

3. ability
4. city
7. family
9. dictionary
10. orderly

Down

1. country
2. party
5. company
6. baby
8. library

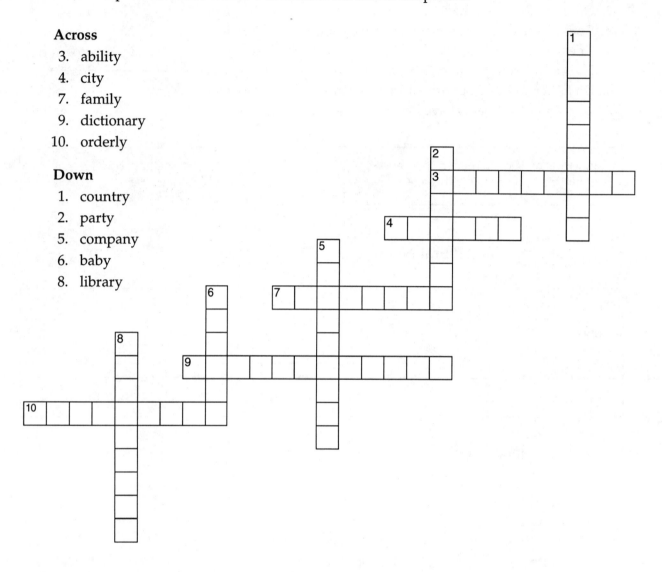

a sink a shower a bath/bathtub a toilet a shower curtain a towel

UNDERSTAND: **Possessive Nouns**

Add apostrophe **s** (**'s**) to nouns to show possession.

> **Tom's** car
> The **teacher's** desk

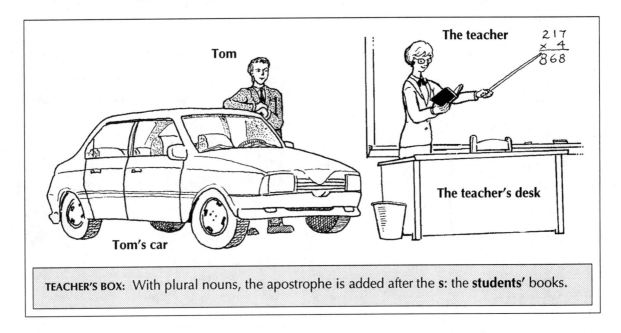

TEACHER'S BOX: With plural nouns, the apostrophe is added after the **s**: the **students'** books.

A. Write the possessive form of the nouns:

classroom / student   **the student's classroom**

1. office / Anne
2. apartment / Chen
3. living room / Joseph
4. house / Roberto
5. brother / Lili
6. glasses / the teacher
7. sister / Nadia
8. camera / Tom
9. daughter / Carla
10. fridge / Yumi

a fridge   a stove   an oven   a counter   a tea kettle   a coffee maker

B. Look at the picture. Whose things are these?

Joseph's walkman

a) suitcase   e) purse   i) keys

b) bicycle   f) soccer ball   j) books

c) sunglasses   g) telephone   k) camera

d) hat   h) guitar   l) tennis racket

Chen   Joseph   Anne   Lili   Roberto

Carla   Yumi   Max   Tom

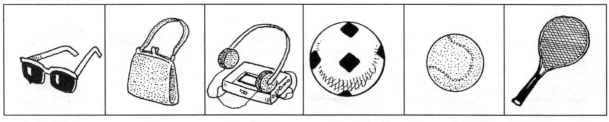

sunglasses   a purse   a walkman   a soccer ball   a tennis ball   a tennis racket

Listening and Speaking: Using Idioms

Do You Have an Apartment for Rent?

A. Practise the expressions with the teacher.

It is smaller than I want.	= **It's too small.**
No, but thank you.	= **Thanks anyway.**

B. Listen and answer the questions.

1. Lili wants to:
   a) rent an apartment
   b) rent a house

2. The apartment has:
   a) three rooms
   b) four rooms
   c) five rooms

3. The apartment has:
   a) one bedroom
   b) two bedrooms
   c) three bedrooms

4. Lili has:
   a) one child
   b) two children
   c) three children

C. Listen and write the words.

Lili: Hello. Do you have _____ apartment for rent?
Landlord: Yes, I do. It has four rooms.
Lili: _____ it have two bedrooms?
Landlord: No, it doesn't. It _____ one bedroom.
Lili: Oh, it's _____ small. I have two kids. Thanks anyway.

an apartment building   a dryer   a clothesline   a clothespin   a dishwasher

D. Practise the conversation with a partner.

I've Got a New Place

A. Practise the expressions with the teacher.

I have	= **I've got**
house, apartment	= **place**
Tell me about it.	= **What's it like?**
Thank you very much.	= **Thanks a lot.**

B. 1. Yumi has a new:
   a) apartment
   b) job

   2. Yumi doesn't have:
   a) a kitchen
   b) a kitchen table

C. Listen and write the words.

Yumi: I've got a new _____.
Anne: That's great. What's it like?
Yumi: It's _____ a nice kitchen, but I don't have a kitchen table.
Anne: Oh, I've got a small table. You _____ have it.
Yumi: Thanks a _____!

D. Practise the conversation with a partner.

Suggestions

Work with a partner. Write a conversation. One person is the owner of the apartment. The other person asks questions about the apartment.

Act out the conversation for the class.

a fan   a vacuum cleaner   an iron   an ironing board   a mop   a broom

Ten-Minute Grammar Games

Mystery Objects

Focus: Practise questions and answers with the verb **have**.

1. Each student puts several small objects into his or her pocket, or holds the items in a closed hand. Suitable items include a few pennies, a paper clip, an eraser, etc.

2. Students work in pairs. They take turns asking questions and responding with short answers:

   Do you have a paper clip?   No, I don't.

   Do you have a pencil?   Yes, I do.

The first student to guess what the other student has is the winner. Students can continue to play, using new objects, for as long as they are interested.

Option: This game can also be played in front of the class, where a student hides something in a box, and other students guess what it is.

Mystery Person

Focus: Review the verb **have** for possessions and descriptions.

1. Review the categories that use the verb **have** or **don't have** (see page 65).

2. Each student writes on a piece of paper the names of five things he or she does or does not have:

   I have a bicycle.

   I have long hair.

   I have two sisters.

   I don't have any brothers.

   I don't have a car.

   They put their papers in a box.

3. Students take turns picking a paper and reading the items on the list. Students guess from the lists who wrote each paper.

Mystery Box

Focus: Practise possessive nouns.

1. Each student contributes three or four objects (e.g., a pencil, an eraser, a ruler) to put in a box.

2. The teacher takes out one object at a time, and asks: "Whose is this?" Students guess, "It's Julio's", "It's Michele's", until they find the owner. When the owner is found, the object is returned.

Option: Students can also take turns pulling objects out of the box and asking the questions.

Test Yourself

Verb "Have"

A. Read the text. Then complete the sentences that follow. Use the verb **have**. Choose the affirmative or negative of **have**:

The hotel **doesn't have** 500 rooms.

Roberto and Carla are at the Holiday Hotel. It is a very big hotel. The hotel has 300 rooms. Roberto and Carla like the hotel. It has a swimming pool and tennis courts. It has five restaurants, a beauty salon, and a gift shop.

The hotel has big rooms and small rooms. Roberto and Carla have a big room. They have a TV and a radio in their room. They also have two telephones and a large bathroom. Their room is very comfortable.

1. The Holiday Hotel _____ a swimming pool.
2. The Holiday Hotel _____ tennis courts.
3. The Holiday Hotel _____ seven restaurants.
4. The Holiday Hotel _____ a shopping centre.
5. The Holiday Hotel _____ different size rooms.
6. Roberto and Carla _____ a small room.
7. Roberto and Carla's room _____ a radio.
8. Roberto and Carla _____ three telephones in their room.
9. Roberto and Carla's room _____ a large bathroom.
10. Roberto and Carla _____ a comfortable room.

B. Complete the sentences. Use the correct form of the verb **have**.

1. _____ you _____ a house or an apartment in Mexico?
2. _____ all the apartments _____ a fridge and stove?
3. Mexico _____ cold weather in winter.
4. Roberto _____ a new car.
5. _____ Roberto and Carla _____ children?
6. The hotel _____ any rooms tonight.
7. _____ this room _____ a shower?
8. Carla _____ any English books.
9. _____ the hotel _____ restaurants?
10. _____ the lobby _____ a desk?

Possessive Nouns

Write sentences. Use possessive nouns. Put the adjectives in the correct place:

camera / new / Ali / expensive / is

Ali's new camera is expensive.

1. walkman / Max / is / small
2. new / glasses / are / the teacher
3. sisters / are / Lili / young
4. friends / nice/ Yumi / are
5. the bus driver / is / job / hard
6. Tom /is / apartment / comfortable
7. children / Carla / are / young
8. brother / is / Anne / tall
9. climate / is / Vancouver / rainy
10. sunglasses / are / Roberto / black

Find the Errors

Which sentences are wrong? Correct the errors.

1. My room doesn't have some towels.
2. She have short hair.
3. We have any friends here.
4. My sister haves two children.
5. They have six suitcases.
6. Our apartment has bigs rooms.
7. Those woman have long hair.
8. The apartment doesn't has furniture.
9. You has free time in the evening.
10. The tourist have a new camera.

7

Present Simple Tense: Affirmative, Negative, Question Form

Pronunciation of Present Tense Verb Endings

Adverbs of Frequency "always," "usually," "often," "sometimes," "never"

Prepositions of Place "in," "on," "under," "between," "beside"

Affirmative	**Negative**		**Contraction**		**Question**	
I walk	I do not		I don't		do I	
you walk	you do not		you don't		do you	
he walks	he does not		he doesn't		does he	
she walks	she does not	walk	she doesn't	walk	does she	walk?
it walks	it does not		it doesn't		does it	
we walk	we do not		we don't		do we	
you walk	you do not		you don't		do you	
they walk	they do not		they don't		do they	

Words You Need

This is Joseph in the morning.

A. Put the pictures in order.

| a take the bus | b leave for work | c get up | d get dressed |
| e eat breakfast | f wake up | g shower | h get to work |

B. Look at the pictures. Write the times.

1. Joseph wakes up: _____
2. He eats breakfast: _____
3. He gets dressed: _____
4. He gets up: _____

5. He takes the bus: _____
6. He leaves for work: _____
7. He showers: _____
8. He gets to work: _____

TEACHER'S BOX: Time is often written with words in expressions such as **five o'clock**, **a quarter to four**, or **half past two**. Numbers may be used for hours past nine: **12 o'clock**. For exact time, numbers are usually used. In this case, parts of the hour are written as minutes, following a colon; for example, **12:35** or **4:15**. Because many North Americans don't use the 24-hour clock, the terms **a.m.** (morning) and **p.m.** (afternoon) are useful.

Understanding Grammar

UNDERSTAND: **Present Simple Tense**

Use the present simple tense to describe things that don't change or actions that are habitual:

The sun **rises** every day.

I **wake up** at seven o'clock.

Affirmative
I walk
you walk
he walks
she walks
it walks
we walk
you walk
they walk

Use the base form of the verb for the present simple tense. Add **s** or **es** to the base form with "he," "she," and "it":

I walk to work.   **She walks to school.**

I go to work.   **She goes to school.**

A. Write the verb.

1. Chen and Lili _____ tea for breakfast. (drink)
2. Max _____ before seven o'clock. (wake up)
3. He _____ in a garage. (work)
4. Yumi _____ to work.(walk)
5. Many people in Vancouver _____ to work. (drive)
6. Anne _____ eggs and toast for breakfast. (eat)
7. Roberto and Carla _____ TV in the evening. (watch)
8. Tom _____ the bus to work. (take)
9. He _____ home with his friend. (go)
10. We _____ to sleep early. (go)

| to wake up | to get up | breakfast | to get dressed | to shower | to take the bus |

B. Look at the pictures. Read about Lili's daily routine. Put the pictures in order.

Lili works hard every day. She gets up at seven o'clock. She makes breakfast for her family at 7:30. She goes to work at 8:30.

Lili is a bank teller. In the morning, she serves people at the bank. She eats lunch at 12 o'clock. In the afternoon, she has meetings and writes letters.

She goes home at 5:30. She eats supper at six o'clock. Then, she watches TV or reads a book. She goes to bed at 11 o'clock.

| to sleep | the sun | sunrise | sunset | tea | toast |

C. Choose the verb. Use the correct form.

walk   leave   eat   watch   drive   get up   finish

Max is a student. He studies English on Wednesday nights. He has a busy schedule. He
_____ early and _____ breakfast. He _____ for work at eight
o'clock. He _____ his car to work.

After work Max _____ to a restaurant near his work. He goes to the English class
near his work too. At nine o'clock the class _____. Max is tired. At home, he
_____ TV.

UNDERSTAND: **Pronunciation of Present Simple Tense Verb Endings**

Use the base form of the verb for the present simple. Add **s** to the base form with "he," "she,"
and "it." For verbs with **ch, sh, x, ss** endings, add **es**. Pronounce the ending /əz/.

Practise with the teacher.

It snows in winter.   He teaches English.
She buys books.   She washes her hands.
He drives to work.   She fixes cars.
He studies hard.   He misses his friends.

UNDERSTAND: **Present Simple Tense Negative**

Use **do not** before the verb. Use **does not** before the verb with **he, she,** and **it**:

I do not live here.
He **does not** live here.

Negative			Contraction		
I do not			I don't		
you do not			you don't		
he does not			he doesn't		
she does not	walk		she doesn't	walk	
it does not			it doesn't		
we do not			we don't		
you do not			you don't		
they do not			they don't		

start/begin   finish/end   to watch (TV)   to study   a schedule   to wash

A. Which sentences are wrong? Correct errors in the verbs.

1. Tom doesn't write letters often.
2. Carla doesn't eats in a restaurant often.
3. Lili and Chen don't walks to work.
4. Yumi don't go to bed early.
5. Carla doesn't cook dinner on Sundays.
6. We doesn't speak Japanese.
7. He doesn't watch TV in the living room.
8. They doesn't talk on the telephone in the mornings.
9. She don't go to movies often.
10. I doesn't work in a store.

B. Write the sentences in the negative. Use contractions:

I like airplanes.   I **don't** like airplanes.

1. Tourists get up early.
2. Nadia and Ali take pictures.
3. They eat dinner at home.
4. He writes letters to his parents.
5. We stay home in the evening.
6. She buys postcards in the hotel.
7. Max walks in the city.
8. Tourists go to bed early.
9. People go to the beach at night.
10. Anne drives the tour bus.

UNDERSTAND: **Present Simple Question Form**

Use **do** or **does** before the subject. Put a question mark (**?**) at the end of the sentence.

Question	
do I	
do you	
does he	
does she	walk?
does it	
do we	
do you	
do they	

to fix/repair   to miss   to drink   to eat lunch   to eat dinner   to buy

A. Make the sentences into questions:

Max wakes up late.   **Does** Max **wake up** late?

1. Tom knows the people in the hotel.
2. She works in the hotel.
3. The tourists meet in the lobby.
4. Anne and Yumi go shopping.
5. Carla takes pictures of the group.
6. The tour begins at two o'clock.
7. We need our keys after 11 o'clock.
8. The restaurant serves good food.
9. Yumi writes to her family.
10. Joseph eats breakfast early.

B. Which sentences are wrong? Correct the errors.

Does Yumi plays the piano? ✘   Does Yumi **play** the piano? ✔

1. Do Nadia and Ali drive to work?
2. Do Max work in a garage?
3. Does she come from Japan?
4. Does Nadia knows Lili?
5. Does Roberto and Carla speak English?
6. Do they get up early?
7. Do we need sunglasses today?
8. Do you works in the hotel?
9. Do your brother speaks English?
10. Does he comes from Korea?

C. Complete the short answers.

Do they play tennis?   No, they don't.

1. Does she work in a hospital?   Yes, she _____.
2. Do you drink coffee?   No, _____ don't.
3. Do we eat lunch in a restaurant? Yes, we _____.
4. Does she take the bus to work?   No, she _____.
5. Do they arrive on time?   Yes, _____ do.
6. Does she go shopping every day? Yes, _____.
7. Do they speak English?   Yes, _____.
8. Do you know my name?   No, I _____.
9. Does the bus leave at 8:30?   No, it _____.
10. Does your camera take good pictures? Yes, _____ does.

to go shopping   to take   to give   to get   to bring   to stay

UNDERSTAND: **Adverbs of Frequency**

always	100%
usually	↑
often	│
sometimes	↓
never	0%

Adverbs of frequency go before the main verb.

Exception: With the verb **be**, they go after the verb:

Some students **always come** to class late.

The weather in Singapore **is never** cold.

A. Which sentences are wrong? Change the adverb if it is in the wrong place:

She never is late for work.   She **is never** late for work.

1. Anne and her sister meet sometimes after work.
2. Nadia usually leaves work at five o'clock.
3. Yumi takes sometimes a taxi to work.
4. They never are late for dinner.
5. The weather in Vancouver sometimes is rainy.
6. Lili always telephones her mother in the morning.
7. Roberto speaks usually Spanish with his family.
8. Max takes often the bus.
9. Anne never leaves work before six.
10. Ali often plays tennis on the weekend.

B. Put the adverb in the correct place in the sentence.

1. People on vacation get up late. (usually)
2. The weather in Thailand is cold. (never)
3. The restaurant serves seafood. (sometimes)
4. Tourists take photographs. (usually)
5. The weather is hot and humid in Panama. (always)
6. The temperature in Montreal changes quickly. (often)
7. People in that hotel are tourists. (usually)
8. We eat before seven. (never)
9. They take pictures of the sunset. (always)
10. He eats in that restaurant. (sometimes)

to clean   to open   to close   to think   to dream   to travel

UNDERSTAND: **Prepositions of Place**

in   on   under   between   beside

A. Look at the picture below. Write the prepositions.

1. The camera is _____ the table.
2. The book is _____ the camera.
3. The woman is _____ the table and the couch.
4. The cat is _____ the box.
5. The TV is _____ the table.
6. The dog is _____ the table.
7. The sunglasses are _____ the camera.
8. The keys are _____ the couch.
9. The apple is _____ the bag.
10. The telephone is _____ the couch.

a shopping bag   on   in   under   between   beside

90

B. Look at the picture. Answer the questions. Write sentences:

Where is the pen? **The pen is under the box.**

1. Where is the pen?
2. Where is the apple?
3. Where is the telephone?
4. Where are the keys?
5. Where is the TV?

6. Where are the pictures?
7. Where is the guitar?
8. Where are the books?
9. Where is the umbrella?
10. Where is the camera?

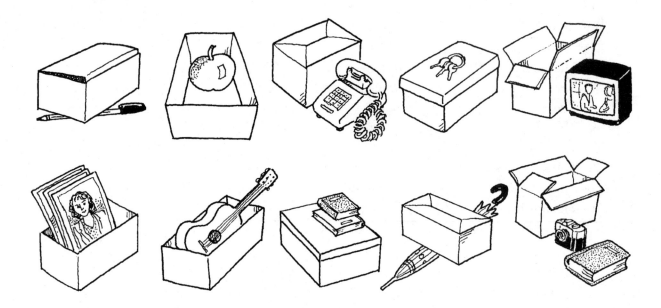

Listening and Speaking: Using Idioms

Does This Bus Go Downtown?

A. Practise the expressions with the teacher.

take it (the bus)	= get it
there	= over there
I'm happy to help.	= No problem.

| a box | to go | to visit | to shake hands | to throw | to catch |

B. Listen and choose the answers.

1. The 129 bus goes downtown.   Yes, it does.   No, it doesn't.
2. The 51 bus goes downtown.   Yes, it does.   No, it doesn't.

C. Listen and write the words.

Max: Excuse _____. Does the 129 bus go downtown?

Bus driver: No it doesn't.

Max: Oh. What bus _____ downtown?

Bus driver: The 51 bus. You _____ it over there.

Max: Thanks a lot.

Bus Driver: _____ problem.

D. Practise the conversation with a partner.

Do You Want a Lift?

A. Practise the expressions with the teacher.

I do too.	= **Me too.**
Do you want to come in my car?	= **Do you want a lift?**

B. Listen and answer the questions.

1. Joseph comes to work by:
   a) train
   b) taxi
   c) bus

2. Max comes to work by:
   a) taxi
   b) car
   c) bus

3. Max and Joseph live:
   a) near school
   b) near the airport
   c) downtown

to stop   to exercise   to run   to jump   to look at   to look for

C. Listen and write the words.

Max: _____ do you come to work every day?

Joseph: I usually take the bus. _____ about you?

Max: I drive to work.

Joseph: Where do you live?

Max: I live downtown.

Joseph: Me _____.

Max: Do you want a _____ sometimes?

Joseph: Sure. Thanks a lot.

D. Practise the conversation with a partner.

Suggestions

Work in pairs. One person is the bus driver. The other person asks for information. Write a conversation.

Act out the conversation for the class.

Ten-Minute Grammar Games

Back and Forth

Focus: Practise questions and answers with present simple tense and adverbs of frequency.

Students work in pairs. Student A asks a question. Student B answers, and then asks Student A a question. The object of the game is to see which pair of students can continue for the longest time.

Student A: Do you take the bus to class?

Student B: No, I don't. I walk to class.

Student B: Do you sometimes eat lunch in a restaurant?

Student A: Yes, I do.

I Spy

Focus: Practise prepositions of place.

1. The teacher reviews prepositions of place (page 89) with the class, and puts the prepositions on the board to help students remember them.

2. To help students remember the phrase they need, the teacher writes on the board, "I spy something that is . . ." The teacher should explain that **spy** means **see**.

3. The teacher starts the game by saying, "I spy something that is near the desk."

4. Students guess what the object is: a chair, a wastepaper basket, etc., until someone answers correctly. The student with the correct answer continues by choosing an object, and saying "I spy something that is . . ."

Find Someone

Focus: Review questions and answers with present simple tense.

1. The teacher writes on the board:

   Do you . . .?   Yes, I do. No, I don't.

2. The aim of the game is to find people who do the activities on the list below. Students walk around the room asking each other questions about their daily habits. When a student answers "Yes", his or her name is written beside the activity. The first person to finish is the winner.

Find someone who:

1. usually eats a big breakfast
2. drinks coffee every morning
3. drinks tea
4. exercises often
5. eats fast food
6. eats lunch in a restaurant
7. usually gets up before seven o'clock
8. sometimes drives to class
9. lives with friends
10. often goes to sleep early
11. cooks supper every day
12. watches TV in the afternoon
13. plays the piano
14. speaks Spanish
15. reads the newspaper in the evening

Test Yourself

Pablo Is From Columbia

A. Complete the story with the verbs. Use the correct form of the present simple.

visit have send come go travel be live like enjoy

Pablo Garcia is from Columbia. He _____ from Bogota. Now he _____ in a small city in Canada. He _____ a job in a car factory in Oshawa. He _____ an engineer. He _____ his job.

Pablo and his family _____ Colombia in the summer. They usually _____ in August. Sometimes they _____ to other places in South America. They _____ their vacation. Pablo _____ postcards to his friends in Oshawa.

B. Answer the questions.

1. What country does Pablo come from?
2. What city does he come from?
3. What city does Pablo live in now?
4. What is Pablo's job?
5. Does Pablo like his job?
6. What does Pablo's family do in the summer?
7. When do they take their vacation?
8. Do they visit other places?
9. Do they enjoy their vacation?
10. What does Pablo send to his friends?

Daily Routine

A. Write questions.

You always get up at seven o'clock.   **Do you always get up at seven o'clock?**

1. You usually watch TV in the evening.
2. Lili always drives to work.
3. Carla and Roberto speak French.
4. Her parents live in a small town.
5. Chen works downtown.
6. I watch TV in the afternoon.
7. Nadia writes to her family.
8. Ali and Tom play tennis after work.
9. They drink tea in the afternoon.
10. Anne wakes up early.

B. Write these sentences in the negative.

Max speaks Japanese.   **Max doesn't speak Japanese.**

1. Lili and her family live in China.
2. Tom leaves for work late.
3. Tourists always eat in restaurants.
4. Roberto goes to bed early.
5. We do homework every night.
6. Ali and Nadia watch TV often.
7. Chen cooks dinner.
8. Max studies very hard.
9. We go to the supermarket every day.
10. They understand Spanish.

Find the Errors

Which sentences are wrong? Correct the errors.

1. He goes sometimes to the beach.
2. We usually eat rice with our meals.
3. It is cold never in Acapulco.
4. Canadians sometimes eat big breakfasts.
5. Hotels give guests keys always.
6. Tourists often go sightseeing.
7. Young people like usually loud music.
8. Students are frequently tired.
9. People on holiday often eat in restaurants.
10. The weather in Canada sometimes is hot.

Where Are They?

Look at the picture on page 95. Write sentences about the objects. Use **near**, **in**, **on**, **under**, **between**, or **beside**.

The camera is on the table.

Vocabulary

Which word is different?

1. breakfast, lunch, juice, supper, dinner
2. morning, evening, spring, night, afternoon
3. hotel, beach, lobby, room, restaurant
4. house, bus, taxi, bicycle, airplane
5. speak, work, drive, keys, drink
6. always, tour, often, sometimes, usually
7. early, late, after, movies, before
8. under, on, always, near, in
9. Hello, 'Bye, See you, late, Hi
10. sunglasses, camera, keys, umbrella, rice

8

Simple Past Tense: Affirmative, Negative, Question Form
Pronouncing Past Tense Endings
Spelling Simple Past Tense Verbs

Affirmative	Negative		Contraction		Question	
I worked	I did not		I didn't		did I	
you worked	you did not		you didn't		did you	
he worked	he did not		he didn't		did he	
she worked	she did not	work	she didn't	work	did she	work?
it worked	it did not		it didn't		did it	
we worked	we did not		we didn't		did we	
you worked	you did not		you didn't		did you	
they worked	they did not		they didn't		did they	

Words You Need

Look at the pictures. Match the actions to the pictures:

answer questions: **k**

1. play the guitar
2. cook a chicken
3. watch TV
4. miss the bus
5. talk to Lili

6. listen to music
7. phone her mother
8. talk to Carla
9. wash his car
10. mail a letter

Understanding Grammar

UNDERSTAND: **Simple Past Tense**

Use the simple past for actions completed in past time:

I **watched** television **last night**.

The expression **last night** shows past time.

TEACHER'S BOX: Because the simple past tense is used for actions that began and ended in past time, it is important that a marker of past time be used or be understood by the context:

I studied hard **last night**.
I studied hard for that exam (**before the exam**).

Irregular past tense forms are covered in Unit 9. See the list of adverbs of past time in Appendix 2 (page 203).

Use **ed** after the verb for the simple past tense:

Affirmative
I worked
you worked
he worked
she worked
it worked
we worked
you worked
they worked

A. Change the verbs to the past tense:

We work hard. **We worked hard.**

1. Chen and Ali walk to the beach.
2. Yumi plays the guitar.
3. The tour guide answers our questions.
4. Max and Roberto talk about soccer.
5. Nadia watches movies on television.

6. The tourists arrive in the morning.
7. Anne listens to the radio.
8. It starts to rain.
9. I telephone my family.
10. Lili turns off the television.

to cook   a chicken   to mail   to call/phone   to listen to   to turn off

B. Choose the verb. Use the past tense.

serve   shout   thank   open   turn on   cook   listen   arrive   end   play

On Saturday we were at a party. It was a surprise party for Max. Max _____ last.
Carla _____ the lights and we _____ "Surprise!" We really surprised Max.

Joseph _____ a chicken. Yumi _____ the chicken with rice and salad. After
dinner, Max _____ his presents. He _____ his friends for the presents.

We _____ games and _____ to Roberto play the guitar. We enjoyed the evening.
The party _____ at midnight.

to turn on   to serve   to shout   to thank   to surprise   a salad

UNDERSTAND: **Pronouncing Simple Past Tense Verb Endings**

Regular Simple Past Tense Verbs (**ed**)		
voiceless consonants	walked watched	pronounce /t/
voiced consonants	played rained	pronounce /d/
verbs ending **t, d**	waited needed	pronounce /əd/

A. Pronounce the past tense with your teacher. Pronounce down and then pronounce across.

Verbs Pronounced /t/	**Verbs Pronounced /d/**	**Verbs Pronounced /əd/**
asked	arrived	added
cooked	closed	counted
finished	enjoyed	ended
helped	opened	needed
stopped	played	started
talked	rained	tasted
worked	smiled	visited
washed	snowed	waited
watched	stayed	wanted

B. Choose the word from each line with the ending /t/.
1. closed, started, worked, needed
2. washed, rained, waited, stayed
3. rained, tasted, asked, arrived
4. smiled, watched, visited, snowed

Choose the word from each line with the ending /d/.
5. counted, cooked, arrived, finished
6. visited, closed, helped, washed
7. worked, visited, played, added
8. needed, closed, asked, talked

presents   midnight   to count   to add   to ask   to answer

Choose the word from each line with the ending /əd/.

9. worked, stayed, talked, wanted
10. finished, enjoyed, needed, smiled
11. stopped, played, started, opened
12. tasted, stopped, played, smiled

UNDERSTAND: **Spelling Simple Past Tense Verbs**

Rules for Spelling Regular Past Tense Verbs			
2 consonants	add **ed**	work	worked
2 vowels + consonant	add **ed**	need	needed
vowel + **y**	add **ed**	play	played
consonant + **y**	change **y** to **i** add **ed**	try	tried
vowel + consonant	double consonant add **ed**	plan	planned

TEACHER'S BOX: Not all verbs that end in vowel + consonant double the final letter. Common exceptions are **listened**, **opened**, **answered**.

A. Write these phrases in the past tense:

work in the bank **worked** in the bank

1. watch TV
2. turn on the light
3. enjoy the movie
4. listen to music
5. stop the cassette
6. try some rice
7. close the window
8. plan a party
9. wait for a taxi
10. call your friend
11. stay at home
12. live in Argentina
13. miss the bus
14. carry a suitcase
15. wash your car
16. study for an exam

to try/taste   to plan   to wait for   to live   to yawn   to shave

B. Which sentences are wrong? Correct wrong spelling of verbs.

1. Yumi **stoped** the cassette before it finished.
2. They **walked** to the beach yesterday.
3. Nadia **waited** for a taxi near the hotel.
4. We **planed** the party for Saturday night.
5. Max **stayed** home and watched TV.
6. Chen **carryed** his wife's suitcase.
7. Roberto **missed** the bus this morning.
8. Carla and Yumi **enjoyed** the movie.
9. Ali **studyed** hard for his exam.
10. Tom and Chen **talked** about cities in Asia.

C. Put the verbs in the simple past tense.
Write them in the crossword puzzle.

Across

3. stop
4. study
7. play
8. carry
10. cry
12. plan

Down

1. walk
2. help
5. enjoy
6. stay
9. miss
11. wait

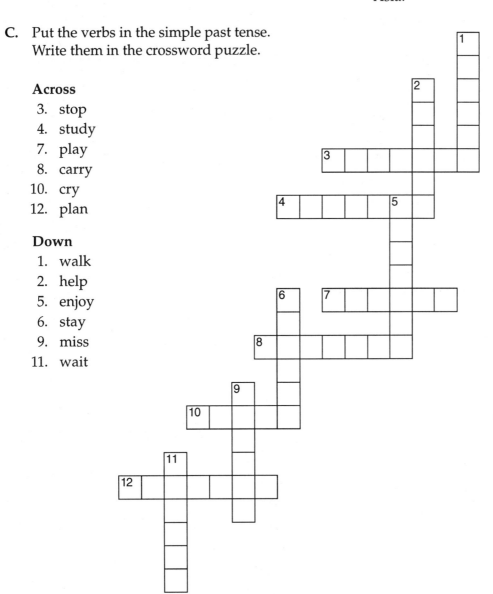

to smile

to laugh

to cry

to need/to want

to make

to learn

UNDERSTAND: **Simple Past Tense Negative**

Use the auxiliary verb **did** + **not**. Use the base form of the main verb:

> We watched TV.   **He did not watch.**

> Wrong   ✗ He did not watched.

Use **did not** for formal communication. Use **didn't** for normal communication. Use **didn't** with singular and plural subjects.

Negative		**Contraction**	
I did not		I didn't	
you did not		you didn't	
he did not		he didn't	
she did not	work	she didn't	work
it did not		it didn't	
we did not		we didn't	
you did not		you didn't	
they did not		they didn't	

A.   Write these sentences in the negative. Use didn't:

We **started** early.   We **didn't start** early.

1. The tourists visited the city.
2. I talked to my friend at breakfast.
3. She liked the food in that restaurant.
4. It rained yesterday.
5. The party ended at 11 o'clock.
6. They played soccer this morning.
7. Nadia and Ali watched TV last night.
8. We arrived at the bus stop on time.
9. Tom carried our suitcases.
10. We talked to the pilot.

| to like | to love | to kiss | to hug | to hold | to fight |

B. This is Joseph's list of things to do. Write sentences about things he didn't do on his list:

He **didn't finish** his homework.

To do: Saturday
✔ phone Roberto
   finish homework
   listen to new cassette
✔ help Tom wash his car
   watch news on TV
✔ play soccer
   finish letter home
   practise piano
✔ cook rice
   go to a movie
   visit friends

UNDERSTAND: **Simple Past Question Form**

Use the auxiliary verb **did** before the subject. Use the base form of the main verb:

You worked late.   **Did** you **work** late?

Wrong   ✗ Did you worked late?

Question	
did I	
did you	
did he	
did she	work?
did it	
did we	
did you	
did they	

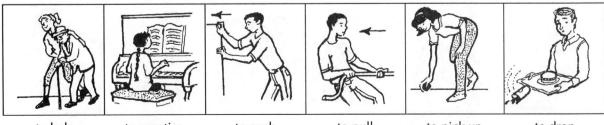

to help   to practise   to push   to pull   to pick up   to drop

A. Write questions:

You cooked dinner.   **Did you cook dinner?**

1. They looked nice.
2. You answered the phone.
3. She asked the question.
4. The bus stopped here.
5. They washed the dishes.

6. I learned Spanish in Mexico.
7. Anne wanted help.
8. He phoned home last night.
9. The bus turned right.
10. They needed a map.

B. Which sentences are wrong? Correct errors in the verbs.

1. Did she phoned home on Tuesday?
2. Did Anne answered my questions?
3. Did the party finish at midnight?
4. Did the tourists wanted help?
5. Did you watched TV yesterday?

6. Did they invite their friends to the party?
7. Did you telephoned me yesterday?
8. Did he need help?
9. Did we wanted music at the party?
10. Did Nadia cook the chicken?

C. Work with a partner. Answer the questions. Use short answers:

Did you learn English in school?   Yes, I did.
                                   No, I didn't.

1. Did you finish your homework last night?
2. Did you arrive at class early this morning?
3. Did you need help with your homework yesterday?
4. Did you walk to class today?
5. Did you telephone a friend last night?
6. Did you telephone your parents yesterday?
7. Did you answer the telephone before breakfast this morning?
8. Did you play the piano yesterday evening?
9. Did you turn on the radio yesterday afternoon?
10. Did you cook any eggs this morning?

a map   to do homework   to set the table   to dust   to iron   to fold

Listening and Speaking: Using Idioms

What Did You Do Yesterday?

A. Practise the expressions with the teacher.

Can I speak to Tom please?	= **Is Tom there please?**
I am speaking.	= **Speaking.**
(To identify yourself on the phone)	= **This is Tom.**
I didn't do anything interesting.	= **Nothing special.**

B. Listen and answer the questions.

1. Who did Tom call?
2. What did Max do yesterday?
3. What did Tom do yesterday?

C. Listen and write the words.

> **Language in Transition**
>
> Formal English would use **whom** rather than **who** in the first question in Exercise B. In current spoken English, **who** is generally used, even for the objective case.

Tom: Hello. Is Max _____ please?

Max: Speaking.

Tom: Hi Max. _____ is Tom. What did you do yesterday?

Max: Yesterday? Oh, nothing _____. I stayed home all day. What _____ you?

Tom: I visited a friend. Then I watched TV at night.

D. Practise the conversation with a partner.

How Was Your Weekend?

A. Practise the expressions with the teacher.

I am tired.	= **I need a rest.**
Wow!	= **Boy!**
Not good, not bad.	= **So so.**

to vacuum   to sweep   to put away   to hit   to sew   to rest

B. Which things did Roberto do on the weekend?

1. washed dishes
2. worked
3. washed the car

4. cleaned the house
5. watched TV
6. listened to music

C. Listen and write the answers.

Anne: Hi Roberto. How was your weekend?

Roberto: So _____. I worked on Saturday.

Anne: Did you finish your work?

Roberto: Yes,_____ did. Then I cleaned the house and washed the car.

Anne: _____! You had a busy weekend.

Roberto: I sure did. Now I need a _____!

D. Practise the conversation with a partner.

Suggestions

Work with a partner. Write a conversation. Begin with "How was your weekend?"
Act out your conversation for the class.

Ten-Minute Grammar Games

Chain

Focus: Practise simple past tense verbs. Review subject pronouns.

This game can be done with the whole class or with smaller groups if the class is large.

1. The teacher begins with a statement in the past tense.

2. Student A repeats and adds on. Student B repeats what was said by the teacher and first student, and adds on:

   Teacher: Yesterday, I watched a movie on TV.

   Student A: Yesterday, she watched a movie on TV. I cleaned the house.

   Student B: Yesterday, she watched a movie; he cleaned the house; I visited friends.

3. Students continue until someone breaks the chain by forgetting or by making a grammatical error.

4. Someone begins a new chain.

Keep track of how long the class can sustain the chain. This game can be repeated at another time, either to review or to practise new structures. Each time, students try to beat their previous class record.

Back and Forth

Focus: Practise asking and answering questions with regular past tense verbs.

1. The teacher reviews question and short answer form for the past tense. The teacher can practise a few questions and answers with the class, and write the questions and answers on the board.

2. Students work in pairs. They can take turns in front of the class or work within larger groups. (If they work in front of the class, they might need some practice time first.)

   Student A asks Student B a question. Student B answers and then asks Student A a question, and so on:

   Student A: What did you do yesterday?
   Student B: I visited my cousin.

   Student B: What did you do yesterday?
   Student A: I talked on the telephone.

3. Students continue in this way until one of them makes a grammatical error. Other students in the class or group should correct the error. When a student makes a mistake, he or she gets a point. Each pair plays for a few minutes. The student with the fewest points wins. Then a second pair of students has a turn. The game continues until everyone in the class has participated.

Test Yourself

Joanna's Story

Read the story. Rewrite it with simple past tense verbs:

Joanna studied English at the University of British Columbia.

Joanna studies English at the University of British Columbia. She likes her class and she works very hard. She has classes four days a week. She doesn't have class on Fridays.

Joanna loves Vancouver and enjoys different activities. Sometimes she walks on the beach. On Saturdays she usually plays tennis. She visits friends and they do their homework together.

Find the Errors

Which sentences are wrong? Correct the errors in the verbs.

1. Max studied hard for his exam.
2. The students enjoied their English class.
3. Yumi planed a trip to Los Angeles.
4. Anne did not liked the new restaurant.
5. The porter carryed the suitcases to the room.
6. Nadia phoned her sister in Florida.
7. Carla learned French in Montreal.
8. The guide did helped the tourists.
9. Anne cook rice for dinner last night.
10. We didn't knew her name.

Max's Terrible Week

Put the negative sentences in the affirmative form.

1. On Monday Max's alarm clock didn't ring.
2. He didn't wake up on time.
3. On Tuesday it didn't rain.
4. Max didn't have an umbrella.
5. Max didn't take his lunch to work.
6. He didn't go out on Friday night.
7. On Saturday he didn't get out of bed early.
8. He didn't know his neighbour's name.
9. He didn't write a letter to his friend.
10. Max didn't think about his homework.

How Was Your Evening?

Use the words. Complete the conversation.

> **Pretty   about   it   watched   so   was   listened   What   was   visited**

Anne: Hi, Yumi. _____ did you do last night?

Yumi: I _____ an old movie on television.

Anne: Was _____ good?

Yumi: So _____. The ending _____ sad. How _____ you? How _____ your evening, Anne?

Anne: _____ good. I _____ my friends and we _____ to music.

Yumi: Are you going to the party tonight?

Anne: Yes. See you soon.

Yumi: Okay. 'Bye.

9

Simple Past Tense Irregular: Affirmative, Negative, Question Form

Prepositions of Time "in," "on," "at"

Spelling Plural Nouns

Simple Past Tense Irregular

bring	brought	begin	began	cost	cost
buy	bought	come	came	find	found
drink	drank	drive	drove	give	gave
eat	ate	fly	flew	know	knew
get	got	go	went	lose	lost
meet	met	leave	left	make	made
sit	sat	send	sent	put	put
sleep	slept	speak	spoke	see	saw
stand	stood	tell	told	sell	sold
take	took	think	thought	wear	wore
write	wrote				

Words You Need

Look at the picture. Match the person and the activity:

sleep under a tree **Max**

1. write a letter
2. eat an apple
3. sleep under a tree
4. buy postcards
5. take a picture
6. stand in line
7. sit at a table
8. drink coffee
9. meet a friend
10. get some cold drinks

Understanding Grammar

UNDERSTAND: **Simple Past Tense Irregular Form**

Use the irregular past tense with these verbs:

bring	brought
buy	bought
do	did
drink	drank
eat	ate
get	got
meet	met
sit	sat
sleep	slept
stand	stood
take	took
write	wrote

> **TEACHER'S BOX:** Many of the most common English verbs have an irregular form in the past tense. Most other verbs in English use the regular form, ending **ed**. Activities in this unit introduce or recycle common past tense verbs. A more complete list of irregular past tense forms can be found in Appendix 3 (page 205).

A. Change the sentences to the past tense:

We take pictures of our friends.   We **took** pictures of our friends.

1. I write to my mother.
2. They drink coffee after dinner.
3. He meets his friend after class.
4. You sit near me in class.
5. We eat in that restaurant.
6. She sleeps in the bus.
7. He brings his homework to class.
8. They buy postcards for their friends.
9. People stand in line at the bank.
10. I get letters from home.

B. Read the paragraphs. Choose the verbs. Write them in the past tense.

bring   take   write   buy   meet   drink   stand   eat   sleep   sit   do

Yesterday afternoon our tour bus was late. We waited for one hour. People in our group _____ different things. Lili and Chen _____ at a table. Lili _____ a letter and Chen _____ coffee. Yumi _____ postcards. Max _____ under a tree.

Roberto _____ a cold drink for Carla. Nadia _____ in line with some other tourists. Anne _____ an apple. Tom _____ a picture. Joseph _____ a friend and talked with her.

to take a picture   to stand   to sit   to meet   a tree

UNDERSTAND: **Simple Past Tense Irregular Negative**

Use the auxiliary verb **did** + **not** before the main verb. **Did** = past tense. Use the base form of the main verb:

> She wrote a letter.   She **did not write** a letter.

Use the contraction **didn't** in normal conversation. Use the full form **did not** to be formal.

Language in Transition

Nowadays, it is common to use contractions for both speaking and informal writing.

Use the irregular past tense with these verbs:

begin	began
come	came
drive	drove
fly	flew
go	went
leave	left
send	sent
speak	spoke
tell	told
think	thought

A. Write the negatives:

The bus left early.   The bus **didn't leave** early.

1. He went to Bali on vacation.
2. They sent us three postcards.
3. Her friend spoke Spanish.
4. We told them our names.
5. I thought it was an old camera.

6. The plane left at eight o'clock.
7. They came from China.
8. Tom drove here from Los Angeles.
9. The tour began at two o'clock.
10. Anne flew here from Paris.

to fly   to send   to tell   to cost   to see   to make

B. Complete the conversation. Use the correct form of the verb.

Lili: We met some interesting people yesterday. They spoke Spanish.

Chen: They didn't _____ (speak) Spanish, Lili. They _____ (speak) Italian.

Lili: Well, they flew here from Madrid.

Chen: They didn't _____ (fly) here from Madrid. They _____ (fly) here from Rome.

Lili: They thought we were Japanese tourists.

Chen: They didn't _____ (think) we were Japanese tourists. They _____ (think) we were Korean.

Lili: Well anyway, I told them that we came here last weekend.

Chen: We didn't _____ (come) here last weekend. We _____ (come) here on Thursday.

Lili: Okay, Chen. You _____ (tell) the story.

UNDERSTAND: **Simple Past Tense Irregular Question Form**

Use **did** before the subject. Use the base form of the main verb:

We swam in the ocean. **Did you swim in the ocean?**

> **TEACHER'S BOX:** The auxiliary verb **did** indicates the past tense, so the main verb is in the base form.

Use the irregular past tense with these verbs:

cost	cost
find	found
give	gave
know	knew
lose	lost
make	made
put	put
see	saw
sell	sold
wear	wore

to swim   to sell   to put   to know   to lose   to find

A. Make questions:

He broke that glass.   **Did he break** that glass?

1. I found some sunglasses in the lobby.
2. They saw their friend in the street.
3. He put the suitcase in the bus.
4. The clerk sold me some flowers.
5. Yumi gave her a present.

6. We wore our raincoats.
7. Robert lost his wallet in the store.
8. The guide knew our names.
9. The bus driver made a left turn.
10. The bus ticket cost one dollar.

B. Which sentences are wrong? Correct the errors.

1. Did your friend said goodbye after the party?
2. The bus didn't left on time.
3. We didn't find Roberto's wallet.
4. Did she told you her name?
5. Did the tourists send any postcards?

6. Where did you put your glasses?
7. The guide didn't tell us his name.
8. They didn't knew our names.
9. I didn't wear my raincoat.
10. Did you speak to her yesterday?

UNDERSTAND: **Prepositions of Time**

Look at the chart.

in	years seasons months	in 1998 in spring in July
on	days of the week weekends dates	on Tuesday on the weekend on July 1, 1995
at	hours minutes	at 12 o'clock at 10:15

to break   to kick   to wear   a wallet   a raincoat   a bus ticket

A. Look at Anne's agenda. Write sentences:

Write the date that Anne's vacation began.   **Anne's vacation began on June 15th.**

1. Write the date that Anne met Yumi.
2. Write the day that Anne got up early.
3. Write the date that she saw the travel agent.
4. Write the date that she made reservations for the hotel.
5. Write the day that she left on her trip.
6. Write the date that she took the train to Vancouver.
7. Write the day that she flew home.
8. Write the date that she sent postcards.
9. Write the day that she bought stamps.
10. Write the date that her vacation finished.

Agenda–Anne Martin   **JUNE**

Sunday	Monday	Tuesday	Wednesday	Thursday	Friday	Saturday
					1	2
3	4	5 See travel agent	6 Get up early	7	8 Make hotel reservations	9
10	11 Buy stamps	12 Meet Yumi	13	14	15 Vacation begins	16 Leave on trip
17 Take train	18 Send postcards	19	20	21	22	23
24 / 31	25	26	27	28	29 Fly home	30 Vacation finished

to say goodbye   an agenda   a vacation   a passport   to check in   security control

B. Write the preposition:

We met **on** July 1, 1978.

1. He lost his wallet _____ the weekend.
2. The tour bus left _____ 8:25 this morning.
3. Yumi wrote her mother _____ Tuesday.
4. Lili and Chen met _____ 1988.
5. Anne sent her postcards _____ Tuesday.
6. We began our trip _____ June 15th.
7. Roberto came to the hotel _____ Friday.
8. They got up _____ seven this morning.
9. Tom took his vacation _____ the spring.
10. We saw our friend in Paris _____ April.

UNDERSTAND: **Plural Nouns with "es"**

Use **es** for the plural of nouns that end with **s, ch, sh, z**:

watch   **watches**

A. Write the plural.

1. camera	5. dish	9. telephone	13. city
2. watch	6. person	10. day	14. box
3. man	7. party	11. family	15. friend
4. child	8. woman	12. glass	16. country

B. Which sentences are wrong? Correct the errors.

1. Yumi looked at some nice watchs.
2. Nadia telephoned her friends yesterday.
3. They visited us for three days.
4. Tom asked about our familys.
5. Carla wore sunglass at the beach.
6. Chen and Tom washed their cars on Saturday.
7. Lili talked with some womans in the park.
8. The tourists wanted to talk about their countrys.
9. We opened the boxes in the lobby.
10. Tom and Ali washed the dishs after the party.

customs   departure lounge   baggage/luggage   a porter   an airplane

Listening and Speaking: Using Idioms

Late for Work

A. Practise the expressions with the teacher.

very bad	= **terrible**
Why?	= **How come?**
angry	= **mad**

B. Listen and answer the questions.

1. Roberto's day was:
   a) good
   b) bad

2. Roberto was:
   a) early for work
   b) late for work

3. Roberto waited for the bus:
   a) 10 minutes
   b) 15 minutes
   c) 20 minutes

4. Roberto's boss was:
   a) sad
   b) angry
   c) happy

C. Listen and write the words.

Max: Hi Roberto. _____ was your day?
Roberto: Terrible. I was late for work this morning.
Max: How _____ ?
Roberto: I missed my bus. Then I waited 20 minutes for the next bus.
Max: _____ your boss angry?
Roberto: Yeah, he was really _____.

D. Practise the conversation with a partner.

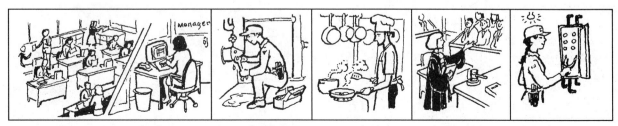

workers   the boss   a plumber   a chef   a lawyer   an electrician

A Terrible Day

A. Practise the expressions with the teacher.

I'm sorrry about it.	= **That's too bad.**
You are lucky.	= **That's lucky.**

B. Listen and answer the questions.

1. Tom's day was:
   a) good
   b) bad

2. Tom's car:
   a) started
   b) didn't start

3. Tom called:
   a) the garage
   b) the store
   c) the school

4. Tom went to work by:
   a) taxi
   b) car
   c) bus

C. Listen and write the words.

Joseph: Hi Tom. How _____ your day?

Tom: Terrible. My car didn't start this morning.

Joseph: That's _____ bad. What did you do?

Tom: I called the garage.

Joseph: How did you _____ to work?

Tom: I got a lift with Roberto.

Joseph: That _____ lucky.

D. Practise the conversation with a partner.

Suggestions

Work with a partner. Write a conversation. Begin with "How was your day?"

Act out your conversation for the class.

a secretary   an accountant   a hairdresser   a factory worker   lucky   unlucky

Ten-Minute Grammar Games

Mystery Box

Focus: Practise past tense verbs and expressions of past time.

1. The teacher writes these time expressions on cards or pieces of paper:

yesterday	last winter
last week	last July
last year	last weekend
last night	yesterday morning
this morning	last Tuesday
last summer	last Saturday

2. Each student picks a card, and says a sentence about something he or she did, using the time expression. If the student says the past tense verb correctly, he or she gets a point. The person with the most points wins.

The Question Game

Focus: Practise questions and answers with irregular past tense verbs.

1. Each student writes the date of his or her birthday, and an activity that he or she did on that date, on a piece of paper:

   January 10: I went to a restaurant.

2. Students work in groups of three or four. Student A tells the group the date on the paper. Other students in the group take turns asking questions to find out what Student A did on that date. Student A answers only, "Yes I did" or "No, I didn't":

Did you watch a movie?	No, I didn't.
Did you go to a restaurant?	Yes, I did!

   When someone guesses correctly, Student A must show his or her paper.

3. The person who guesses the activity correctly is the winner. Then he or she takes a turn answering questions. If no one guesses correctly after about ten questions, Student A gives the answer and then chooses someone else to take a turn.

Test Yourself

Tom's Vacation

A. Use the correct form of the verbs. Use the simple past tense.

Tom's vacation _____ (be) last August. He _____ (go) to Venezuela with a friend. They really _____ (enjoy) their trip. They _____ (be) there for two weeks. They _____ (try) different things to eat and drink. They _____ (eat) some delicious food.

At the hotel they _____ (meet) some people with a car and they _____ (drive) to some beautiful beaches. They _____ (take) pictures and _____ (buy) souvenirs. Tom _____ (send) postcards to his family and friends in Los Angeles.

B. Answer the questions. Use complete sentences:

When did Tom go on vacation?   **He went in August.**

1. Where did Tom go on vacation?
2. Did Tom go alone?
3. Did he and his friend enjoy the trip?
4. Did they stay in Venezuela long?
5. Was the food good?
6. Where did they stay?
7. Where did they drive to?
8. Did they take pictures?
9. What did they buy?
10. What did Tom send to his friends?

On the Road

Write the negative:

We left at nine o'clock.   **We didn't leave at nine o'clock.**

1. We flew from London to Paris.
2. They took the boat from London to New York.
3. She went to London on business.
4. People stood in line to get tickets.
5. He thought the train was comfortable.
6. That woman lost her ticket.
7. The porter spoke English.
8. We got our tickets at the airport.
9. They told stories about their trip.
10. They bought souvenirs in Hong Kong.

Questions and Answers

Write questions with **what**:

What **did Yumi drink?** Yumi drank tea.

1. What _____? Roberto ate spaghetti.
2. What _____? Carla bought postcards.
3. What _____? Anne said goodbye.
4. What _____? Ali drank coffee.
5. What _____? Max lost his wallet.

Prepositions

Which preposition is correct?

(in) summer   on summer

1. in 1993	on 1993
2. on July	in July
3. at winter	in winter
4. in weekends	on weekends
5. at Monday	on Monday
6. on March 5	in March 5
7. in summer	on summer
8. on two o'clock	at two o'clock
9. at 7:15	in 7:15
10. on May 1	at May 1

Find the Errors

Which verb is not correct?

1. arrived   waited   talked   enjoied   stayed
2. standed   looked   watched   answered   listened
3. played   buyed   studied   cried   called
4. phoned   cooked   missed   drinked   found
5. washed   talked   brang   opened   closed

Adverbs of Frequency: Daily Activities

A. Think about your daily routine. Put a check (✔) in the right place.

	Always	Usually	Often	Sometimes	Never
eat a big breakfast					
drink coffee with sugar					
arrive late in class					
do homework					
take the bus					
walk to school					
eat fish for dinner					
wake up late					
watch TV after dinner					
go to bed early					

B. Write sentences about these activities. Use adverbs of frequency:

I never eat a big breakfast.

1. eat breakfast
2. drink coffee
3. take a taxi
4. do homework
5. take the bus
6. go to school
7. eat chicken for supper
8. arrive early
9. go out after dinner
10. go to bed early
11. shop for clothes
12. watch a movie

Simple Past Tense

A. Look at Nadia's schedule. It is Sunday night. Answer the questions:

When did Nadia watch a movie?   **She watched a movie Saturday afternoon.**

Nadia's Schedule			
	Friday	**Saturday**	**Sunday**
9-12	finish letter	clean the house	wash the car
1-5	work in the office	watch movie	visit friends
7-10	talk on the phone	listen to music	

1. When did Nadia watch a movie?
2. When did Nadia wash the car?
3. When did Nadia clean the house?
4. When did Nadia work in the office?
5. When did Nadia listen to music?

B. Answer the questions:

What did Nadia do yesterday afternoon?   **She watched a movie.**

1. What did Nadia do yesterday morning?
2. What did Nadia do Friday night?
3. What did Nadia do Friday morning?
4. What did Nadia do this afternoon?
5. What did Nadia do Saturday night?

Simple Past Tense Irregular Form

A. Read the letter. Answer the questions.

Dear Ana Luisa,

We arrived at the hotel yesterday at six o'clock. We took a bus from the airport to the hotel. We have a nice room. Our room is near the swimming pool. We didn't swim last night. We were hungry after the trip. We ate dinner in the restaurant. We met some people at the next table. They were from Canada. We drank coffee with them after dinner.

Carla and Roberto

1. When did Carla and Roberto arrive at the hotel?
2. How did they get from the airport to the hotel?
3. Where is their room?
4. Did they use the swimming pool last night?
5. When were they hungry?
6. Where did they eat dinner?
7. Did they meet any people?
8. Where were the people from?
9. What did they drink after dinner?

B. Complete the chart.

	began	meet	met
bring	brought	put	
	bought	say	said
come	came		saw
cost		sell	sold
	did		sent
drink	drank	sit	sat
drive	drove	sleep	slept
eat		speak	
	found	stand	stood
fly	flew	swim	swam
get			took
give	gave	tell	told
go		think	
	knew	understand	
lose	lost	wear	wore
	made		wrote

C. Work with a partner. Put the verbs in the past tense. Write them in the crossword puzzle.

Across	Down
1. sit	1. stand
2. sleep	2. see
3. swim	3. send
4. drink	5. eat
6. write	6. wear
7. make	7. meet
8. tell	9. do

Spelling

Fill in the missing letters

1. I sw__m in the swimming pool last night.
2. They enjo__ed the party at Yumi's.
3. Roberto dr__nk coffee after dinner.
4. Yumi and Anne come from small famili__s.
5. We __te dinner in a restaurant last night.
6. Lili and Nadia bou__ht some postcards.
7. Where did he put his ke__s?
8. Max c__me to class late yesterday.
9. Joseph to__k some pictures of his friends.
10. Tom and Ali come from big cit__es.

Questions with "How" and "Where"

Read the story. Complete the information in the chart.

Last month Tom had a family reunion. People in his family came to the hotel for a week. Tom's parents flew in from Los Angeles. His sister drove in from San Diego. His cousin took the train from Winnipeg. His grandparents took the bus from Portland. Tom's brother came by ferry and bus. He came from Victoria.

Relatives	How did they come?	Where did they come from?
parents		
	drove	
		Winnipeg
	bus	
brother		

11

Count and Non-Count Nouns
"There" + "Be": Affirmative, Negative, Question Form
Imperatives

There + Be		
there **is + a**	singular count nouns	There **is a** glass on the table.
there **is + some**	non-count nouns	There **is some** butter on the table.
there **are + some**	plural count nouns	There **are some** glasses on the table.

There + Be Negative		
there **is not + any**	non-count nouns	There **isn't any** butter on the table.
there **are not + any**	plural count nouns	There **aren't any** glasses on the table.

There + Be Question Form		
is there + **a**	singular count noun	**Is** there **a** glass on the table?
is there + **any**	non-count nouns	**Is** there **any** butter on the table?
are there + **any**	plural count nouns	**Are** there **any** glasses on the table?

Words You Need

Match the words to the pictures.

1. an oven
2. a table
3. a counter
4. a refrigerator
5. a stove
6. some glasses
7. some plates

8. some cups
9. a bowl
10. a drawer
11. a knife
12. a fork
13. a spoon
14. a chicken

15. an egg
16. potatoes
17. a carrot
18. onions
19. an apple
20. an orange
21. a tomato

Understanding Grammar

UNDERSTAND: **Count and Non-count Nouns**

Singular count nouns follow the article **a** or **an** (a tomato, an egg). Plural count nouns follow **some** (some eggs) or Ø article (eggs).

A. Write **a**, **an**, or **some**.

1. apple
2. eggs
3. bowl
4. knife
5. carrot
6. onions
7. refrigerator
8. spoons
9. orange
10. plate
11. glasses
12. apples
13. kitchen
14. oven
15. sandwiches
16. oranges
17. egg
18. plates
19. onion
20. glass

Non-count nouns don't have a singular form. They follow **some** (**some sugar**).

TEACHER'S BOX: Some nouns are non-count in English, but count in other languages. Common examples are baggage, money, spaghetti, hair, information, and news. These nouns may confuse some students who will want to use an article:

✗ some hairs, an information

English uses partitives to designate quantity with non-count nouns:

a piece of bread, a cup of sugar.

For a list of common partitives, see Appendix 1 (page 201).

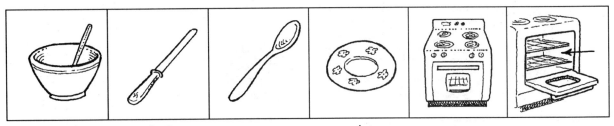

a bowl   a knife   a spoon   a plate   a stove   an oven

B. Put the words in the chart.

1.	meat	11.	knife
2.	eggs	12.	water
3.	spaghetti	13.	banana
4.	glasses	14.	plates
5.	orange	15.	salt
6.	cereal	16.	onions
7.	tomato	17.	fruit
8.	rice	18.	lettuce
9.	spoons	19.	cups
10.	oven	20.	sugar

Count	Non-count

meat   an orange   cereal   a tomato   a banana   an onion

C. Put **a**, **an**, or **some** before count nouns. Put **some** before non-count nouns.

1. _____ egg
2. _____ tomato
3. _____ bread
4. _____ coffee
5. _____ sugar
6. _____ table
7. _____ apple
8. _____ salt
9. _____ banana
10. _____ milk

11. _____ potatoes
12. _____ muffins
13. _____ forks
14. _____ water
15. _____ stove
16. _____ spoons
17. _____ refrigerator
18. _____ rice
19. _____ butter
20. _____ glass

UNDERSTAND: **"There" + "Be"**

Use **there** + **be** to describe things.

"There" + "Be"		
there **is** + **a**	singular count nouns	There **is a** glass on the table.
there **is** + **some**	non-count nouns	There **is some** butter on the table.
there **are** + **some**	plural count nouns	There **are some** glasses on the table.

fruit   lettuce   a carrot   an apple   a sandwich   an egg

A. Put **There is** or **There are** in the sentences. Use the chart on page 133 to help you.

1. _____ a glass in the cupboard.
2. _____ some glasses on the table.
3. _____ some sugar in my coffee.
4. _____ a spoon in the bowl.
5. _____ some forks near the plate.
6. _____ some bread on the counter.
7. _____ some butter in the refrigerator.
8. _____ a chicken in the oven
9. _____ some soup on the stove.
10. _____ some eggs in the refrigerator.

B. Look at the picture of the refrigerator. Answer the question, "What's in the refrigerator?" Make a list:

There are some eggs.

| bread | coffee | sugar | salt | milk | water |

UNDERSTAND: "**There**" + "**Be**" Negative

"There" + "Be" Negative		
there **are not** + **any**	plural count nouns	There **aren't any** glasses on the table.
there **is not** + **any**	non-count nouns	There **isn't any** butter on the table.

> **TEACHER'S BOX:** The alternative and less common way to express negatives with **there + be** is with the form **there is no** or **there are no**. This form is generally used for emphasis.
> There is no sugar in the coffee. There are no apples left.

A. Write the negative form of these sentences.

1. There is some bread on the counter.
2. There are some apples on the table.
3. There is some butter in the sandwich.
4. There are some tomatoes in this sandwich.
5. There is some sugar in my tea.
6. There are some apples at the supermarket.
7. There are some sandwiches on the table.
8. There are some oranges in that bowl.
9. There is some milk in the refrigerator.
10. There is some coffee in this cup.

B. Put **There isn't** or **There aren't** in the sentences.

1. _____ any milk on the table.
2. _____ any oranges in that bowl.
3. _____ any salt in the soup.
4. _____ any butter on my bread.
5. _____ any sugar in his coffee.
6. _____ any eggs in the refrigerator.
7. _____ any tomatoes on the counter.
8. _____ any fish in the store.
9. _____ any plates on the table.
10. _____ any cups in the cupboard.

| a lemon | soup | a potato | a muffin | butter | a refrigerator |

UNDERSTAND: "**There**" + "**Be**" Question Form

Put the verb **be** before **there**. Use **any** after **there** to ask questions.

"There" + "Be" Question Form		
is there + **a**	singular count nouns	**Is** there **a** glass on the table?
is there + **any**	non-count nouns	**Is** there **any** butter on the table?
are there + **any**	plural count nouns	**Are** there **any** glasses on the table?

A. Make questions:

There is **some** sugar in his tea.   Is there **any** sugar in his tea?

1. There is a chicken on the stove.
2. There are some oranges in that bag.
3. There are potatoes with the chicken.
4. There is a spoon on the counter.
5. There are some forks in that drawer.
6. There is some lettuce in that sandwich.
7. There is a cup on the table.
8. There are some apples in the refrigerator.
9. There are some glasses in the cupboard.
10. There is some milk in my coffee.

B. Look at the picture on page 137. Answer the questions with short answers:

Is there a glass on the table? **Yes, there is.**

1. Is there any sugar on the table?
2. Is there a chicken in the refrigerator?
3. Is there any coffee on the stove?
4. Are there any eggs in the refrigerator?
5. Are there any plates on the table?
6. Are there any spoons on the table?
7. Is there a bowl on the table?
8. Are there any apples in the bowl?
9. Is there any salt on the table?
10. Is there any milk in the refrigerator?

> **TEACHER'S BOX:** It is possible to use **some** with the question form when a positive answer is expected.

a cupboard   a drawer   fish   tea   a glass   a bag

UNDERSTAND: **Imperatives**

Use the imperative to give directions, instructions, or warnings. Use the base form of the verb for the imperative. Use **don't** and the base form of the verb for the negative form.

Directions:	**Add salt and pepper.**
Instructions:	**Don't forget the eggs.**
Warnings:	**Be careful. It's hot.**

pepper	to be careful	to add	mayonnaise	cheese	yoghurt

A. Match the sentences to the pictures.

1. Wait. It's too hot.
2. Don't put in any sugar, please.
3. Try this cake.
4. Don't eat too fast.
5. Have some fruit.
6. Please sit here.

B. Read the directions to make a cheese sandwich. Put the steps in order.

a) Spread the butter on one piece of bread.
b) Cut the sandwich in half.
c) Eat the sandwich.
d) Put cheese on the bread.
e) Get some bread, butter, and cheese.
f) Put a piece of bread on top.

fast   slow   to cut   to spread   a cake   a pie

UNDERSTAND: **"Let's" for Suggestions**

Use **let's** + the base form of the verb to make suggestions in the imperative:

Let's go to the supermarket.

Match the statement on the left with the suggestion on the right:

It is Roberto's birthday.   Let's have a party.

1. This room is very hot.	a) Let's go to the store.
2. Max and Ali like soft drinks.	b) Let's make tea.
3. She can't speak Spanish.	c) Let's eat fish.
4. We don't have any fish.	d) Let's stay at home.
5. Yumi is a good cook.	e) Let's take the car.
6. We are hungry.	f) Let's speak English.
7. The store is far from here.	g) Let's open the window.
8. I don't like coffee.	h) Let's eat dinner.
9. I'm really tired tonight.	i) Let's buy some coke.
10. She doesn't eat meat.	j) Let's ask her to make dinner.

Listening and Speaking: Using Idioms

What's For Supper?

A.   Practise the expressions with the teacher.

What are we having for supper?	= **What's for supper?**
to warm the food	= **to heat it up**
Are there other things . . .?	= **Is there anything else?**

a birthday party   a soft drink   juice   ice cream   a doughnut

B. Listen and answer the questions.

Which things are in the fridge?

1. an egg
2. some chicken
3. a potato
4. some rice
5. some fish
6. an apple
7. some salad

C. Listen and write the words.

Ali: Nadia, I'm hungry. What's _____ supper?

Nadia: Well, there's some chicken in the fridge.

Ali: Is there _____ rice?

Nadia: Yes, there is. There's some in a bowl. I can heat it _____.

Ali: Is there anything _____ in the fridge?

Nadia: Yes, there's some salad.

D. Practise the conversation with a partner.

What a Great Party!

A. Practise the expressions with the teacher.

This is a (great party)!	= **What a** (great party)!
Let's eat (the chicken).	= **Let's** try (the chicken).
I am very hungry.	= **I'm starving.**
Let's go.	= **Come on.**

a hot dog   pizza   a hamburger   french fries   egg rolls   to heat

B. Listen and write the words.

Max: _____ a great party! The food looks delicious.

Tom: Let's _____ the chicken. It looks really good.

Max: What's for dessert?

Tom: There's a chocolate cake.

Max: _____ starving. Come _____. Let's eat!

C. Practise the conversation with a partner.

Suggestions

Work with a partner. Write a conversation. Begin with "I'm starving. What's for supper?" Act out your conversation for the class.

Ten-Minute Grammar Games

Any Suggestions?

Focus: Practise using the expression **Let's** and imperatives.

1. The class brainstorms a list of situations such as "I'm hungry", "I'm tired", "I'm cold." The teacher writes them on the board.

2. Students work in groups. They are given a time limit, and asked to come up with as many suggestions as they can, beginning with **Let's**. The group with the most suggestions, or with the most creative suggestions, wins.

Mystery Box

Focus: Review articles with count and non-count nouns.

1. Each student contributes three or four objects (e.g., a pencil, an eraser, a ruler) and puts them in a box.

2. The teacher picks up one or more objects, but does not show the class. The teacher asks, "What's in my hand?"

Students guess: "There are some paper clips", "There's an eraser", etc. When they guess correctly, using correct grammar, the object is returned to its owner.

Option: Students can take turns picking things up from the box and calling "What's in my hand?"

Test Yourself

Count/Non-count Nouns

A. Put the nouns in the correct column.

1. a chicken
2. a banana
3. some money
4. some news
5. a cup
6. some soup
7. a stove
8. an egg
9. some sugar
10. some spoons
11. some bread
12. some potatoes
13. some plates
14. a glass
15. some rice
16. an orange
17. some butter
18. a tomato
19. some salt
20. forks

Count singular	Count plural	Non-count

B. Write **a, an,** or **some.**

1. plates	8. table	15. cup
2. apple	9. fridge	16. spoon
3. chairs	10. bread	17. bowls
4. knife	11. oven	18. egg
5. glass	12. tomatoes	19. apples
6. orange	13. onions	20. fork
7. eggs	14. sandwiches	

In the Kitchen

A. Write **is** or **are.**

1. _____ there any water in the fridge?
2. There _____ some oranges in the fruit bowl.
3. _____ there any hot food on the table?
4. _____ there any people in the kitchen?
5. There _____ some eggs for breakfast.
6. _____ there any cheese to make a sandwich?
7. There _____ a chicken in the oven.
8. There _____ some sugar in the coffee.
9. There _____ some glasses on the counter.
10. _____ there any meat with the potatoes?

B. Write a sentence with the imperative form:

You need the milk for your coffee. (pass / milk) **Please pass the milk.**

1. You want your little brother to eat slowly. (eat / slowly)
2. You want your friend to add salt to the food. (add / salt)
3. You want your brother to put butter on the table. (put / butter)
4. You want your sister to have some dessert. (have / dessert)
5. You don't want your friend to be late. (be / late)

C. Make suggestions:

We are very tired. Let's (bed / go) **Let's go to bed.**

1. We don't have any milk. Let's (store / go)
2. We are hungry. Let's (dinner / have)
3. We don't like tea. Let's (coffee / drink)
4. We don't have any glasses. Let's (cups / use)
5. We are too hot. Let's (window / open)

Spelling

Fill in the missing letters.

1. chi__ken
2. fri__ge
3. wat__r
4. potat__es
5. brea__fast
6. on__on
7. san__wich
8. che__se
9. glass__s
10. k__ife

11. s__oon
12. kit__hen
13. lett__ce
14. ban__na
15. oran__e
16. cof__ee
17. bo__l
18. refri__erator
19. ap__les
20. ov__n

<table>
<tr><td>

12

</td><td>

Present Continuous Aspect: Affirmative, Negative, Question Form

Spelling Verbs Ending with "ing"

Possessive Pronouns "mine," "his," "hers," "its," "ours," "yours," "theirs"

Questions with "Whose"

</td></tr>
</table>

Affirmative

I am	
you are	
he is	
she is	eating
it is	
we are	
you are	
they are	

Contraction

I'm	
you're	
he's	
she's	eating
it's	
we're	
you're	
they're	

Negative

I am not	
you are not	
he is not	
she is not	eating
it is not	
we are not	
you are not	
they are not	

Question

am I	
are you	
is he	
is she	eating?
is it	
are we	
are you	
are they	

Contraction

I'm not	
you're not	
he's not	
she's not	eating
it's not	
we aren't	
you aren't	
they aren't	

Words You Need

Match the pictures to the words.

1. shoes
2. a jacket
3. jeans
4. a T-shirt
5. pants
6. a coat

7. a dress
8. a sweater
9. a hat
10. a shirt
11. a skirt
12. a blouse

Understanding Grammar

UNDERSTAND: **Present Continuous Aspect**

Use the present continuous for actions that are in progress now:

I'm eating an apple right now.

Use the present continuous for temporary situations:

They **are travelling** in South America at the moment.

To form the present continuous, put the auxiliary verb **be** before the main verb. Add **ing** to the verb. The ending **ing** shows continuous action. The auxiliary **am**, **is**, or **are** shows present time.

Affirmative		Contraction	
I am		I'm	
you are		you're	
he is		he's	
she is	eating	she's	eating
it is		it's	
we are		we're	
you are		you're	
they are		they're	

TEACHER'S BOX: The continuous aspect tells **how** an action takes place. Only verbs that show action (dynamic verbs) can have continuous aspect:

Wrong: ✘ I am knowing your name.
         ✔ I know your name.

Some common verbs that do not show action (stative verbs) are **believe**, **know**, **hate**, **hear**, **like**, **love**, **need**, **own**, **see**, **seem**, **understand**, **want**.

The verb **have** generally has a stative meaning. However, it has a dynamic meaning in phrases such as "I am having fun", "They are having coffee now", "We are having a good time at this party", "She is having lunch with her friend." Other languages may not use **have** in this way, so students may learn these phrases best as expressions.

shoes	a jacket	jeans	a T-shirt	pants	a coat

A. Look at the pictures. Match the questions to the answers.

1. What is Lili doing?
2. What is Anne doing?
3. What is Tom doing?
4. What is Nadia doing?
5. What is Max doing?
6. What is Joseph doing?
7. What are Carla and Roberto doing?

a) He's looking for a jacket.
b) She's trying on shoes.
c) She's waiting in line.
d) He is looking at T-shirts.
e) He's trying on a coat.
f) She's looking at dresses.
g) They are buying jeans.

a dress   a sweater   a hat   a shirt   a skirt   a blouse

B. Which sentences are wrong? Correct errors in the verbs:

Roberto _∧^{is} buying some jeans.

1. Nadia and Anne shopping in a shoe store.

2. Lili is buying a new dress.

3. Roberto are trying on sunglasses.

4. Chen paying with his credit card.

5. Yumi is looking for a new jacket.

6. I shopping in the same store.

7. Tom is waiting in line to pay for his shirt.

8. Max and Joseph is leaving the store.

9. Nadia carrying a shopping bag.

10. A clerk is putting Yumi's jacket into a bag.

C. Choose the verb and put it in the present continuous.

talk   wait   help   sell   pay   buy   try on

Today the department store is having a sale. They _____ coats and dresses for 50 percent off. Nadia is shopping for a new coat. Anne _____ her find a coat.

Lili and Carla are also at the department store. Carla _____ a dress. Lili _____ in line to pay for a new blouse. A woman near her _____ to a friend. They _____ some T-shirts. They _____ for them with a credit card.

D. Read the story again. Answer the questions.

1. Who is selling coats and dresses?
2. Who is shopping for a coat?
3. Who is helping Nadia?
4. Where are Lili and Carla?

5. What is Carla trying on?
6. What is Lili buying?
7. What are the women buying?
8. How are they paying?

to look for   to try on   to buy   to pay    a credit card    cash

UNDERSTAND: **Spelling Verbs Ending with "ing"**

Spelling Verbs Ending with "ing"		
verbs that end with **e**	drop **e**, add **ing**	write writing
verbs that end with two consonants, two vowels, or two vowels and a consonant	add **ing**	try trying see seeing read reading
verbs that end with a vowel and a consonant	double final letter add **ing**	put putting

TEACHER'S BOX: The spelling rules for continuous verbs are different from the rules for regular past tense verbs. For example, with the verb **try**, the past tense is **tried**, but the continuous form is **trying**. This may lead to some confusion when students are learning the forms.

A. Write these sentences in the present continuous:

They shop. **They are shopping.**

 1. We eat dinner late.
 2. I wake up early.
 3. He studies hard.
 4. They get off the bus.
 5. You sit in the bus.
 6. He puts his wallet into his pocket.
 7. I smile at my friends.
 8. We read in the library.
 9. She waits for the bus near home.
 10. They work for the bank.

a department store   a sale   a suit   a tie   pyjamas

B. Write the continuous form of the these verbs. Put them in the crossword puzzle.

Across
3. leave
6. have
7. shop
8. carry
9. talk

Down
1. help
2. pay
4. get
5. wear
7. sit

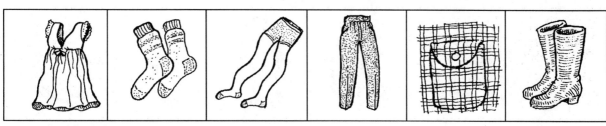

a nightgown   socks   pantyhose   pants   a pocket   boots

152

UNDERSTAND: **Present Continuous Negative**

Use **not** after the auxiliary verb **be**. Use the **ing** form of the main verb:

He **is not** eating right now.

Negative		
I am not		
you are not		
he is not		
she is not	eating	
it is not		
we are not		
you are not		
they are not		

Contraction		
I'm not		
you're not		
he's not		
she's not	eating	
it's not		
we aren't		
you aren't		
they aren't		

TEACHER'S BOX: An auxiliary verb is used to show time, person, or negation. The main verb is used to indicate aspect.

Simple aspect is shown by the base form of the main verb and the auxiliary **do**; e.g., He **doesn't eat** fish. Continuous aspect is shown by using the **ing** form of the verb and the auxiliary **be**; e.g., He **is not eating** fish right now.

A. Write the sentences in the present continuous. Use the negative form. Use contractions:

They eat fish on Fridays. (tonight) **They aren't eating fish tonight.**

1. Joseph often takes pictures. (this afternoon)
2. Anne usually eats alone. (tonight)
3. Chen sometimes talks to the bus driver. (now)
4. Max always watches TV in the morning. (this morning)
5. Nadia and Carla often play tennis. (today)
6. Yumi always smiles at the camera. (at the moment)
7. Tom and Roberto usually wear jeans. (right now)
8. Lili frequently wears a sweater in the evening. (this evening)
9. Anne and Yumi often have coffee in that cafe. (at the moment)
10. Ali and Nadia usually listen to the news after dinner. (tonight)

B. Look at the pictures on page 153. Use the present continuous negative form to correct the information:

She is wearing a T-shirt. **She isn't wearing a T-shirt. She's wearing a raincoat.**

1. Chen and Lili are buying T-shirts.
2. Yumi is trying on a dress.
3. Roberto is looking at jackets.
4. Joseph is wearing a shirt.
5. Ali and Nadia are carrying coats.
6. Carla is holding a blouse.

  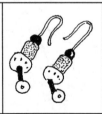  

| a bathing suit | a bikini | a necklace | earrings | a bracelet | a ring |

UNDERSTAND: **Present Continuous Question Form**

Use the auxiliary verb to form questions. Put the auxiliary verb **be** before the subject. The main verb uses the **ing** form. Put a question mark (**?**) at the end of the sentence:

Tom is wearing his hat today.   **Is Tom wearing** his hat today**?**

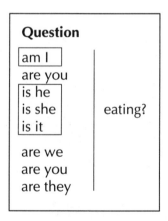

Question

am I	
are you	
is he	
is she	eating?
is it	
are we	
are you	
are they	

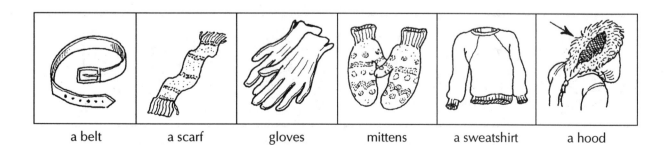

a belt   a scarf   gloves   mittens   a sweatshirt   a hood

A. Change the statements to questions:

Max is taking pictures. **Is Max taking pictures?**

1. You are sleeping.
2. We are looking for Tom.
3. Yumi is writing to her sister.
4. He is wearing new shoes.
5. They are waiting for the bus.
6. Nadia is trying on that jacket.
7. You are visiting the city.
8. Anne is carrying that big suitcase alone.
9. Tom and Roberto are speaking Spanish.
10. You are looking for her glasses.

B. Which sentences are wrong? Correct the errors.

1. Max is listening to music?
2. Are Yumi and Anne eating fish?
3. Is she watch a movie?
4. Nadia and Ali are eating lunch now?
5. You are buying postcards for your family?
6. Are you waiting for a friend?
7. Is Roberto having a good time at the party?
8. Is Lili shopping for shoes?
9. Tom is having dinner in a restaurant?
10. Are you talking to me?

UNDERSTAND: **Possessive Pronouns**

Possessive pronouns show ownership. They have the same gender (male, female) as the owner. Possessive pronouns replace possessive adjective + noun:

This is **her dress**. This is **hers**.

These are **his jeans**. These are **his**.

Possessive pronouns often answer the question **Whose**:

Whose coat is this? It's **his**.

Whose shoes are these? They're **hers**.

This dress is hers.   **These jeans are his.**

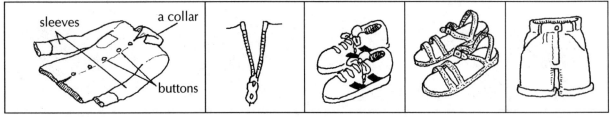

a shirt   a zipper   running shoes   sandals   shorts

Possessive Adjectives		Possessive Pronouns
my key	my keys	mine
your key	your keys	yours
his key	his keys	his
her key	her keys	hers
its key	its keys	✘
our key	our keys	ours
your key	our keys	yours
their key	our keys	theirs

Mine

TEACHER'S BOX: English nouns do not generally have grammatical gender. Pronouns agree in number and gender with the owner of the object, not with the object itself. **Its** doesn't occur as a possessive pronoun. The English pronoun system is inconsistent and difficult for students from many language groups.

A. Write the possessive pronoun:

my coat **mine**

her shoes **hers**

1. his wallet
2. our car
3. their suitcase
4. my sunglasses
5. your camera
6. her keys

B. Choose the correct pronoun.

1. This is _____ (my/mine) friend.
2. Those books are _____ (her/hers).
3. _____ (Our/Ours) teacher is tall.
4. Where are _____ (your/yours) brothers?
5. Are they visiting _____ (my/mine) house?
6. Is that jacket _____ (him/his)?
7. _____ (Their/theirs) teacher works hard.
8. These are _____ (my/mine).
9. Where are _____ (your/yours)?
10. They are helping _____ (their/theirs) friends.

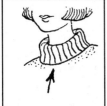     

a turtleneck   a uniform   a bathrobe   a schoolbag   a briefcase   a watch

C. Use possessive pronouns to answer the questions:

Whose picture is that? (Yumi's)   **It's hers.**

Whose glasses are those? (Ali's)   **They're his.**

1. Whose keys are those? (Anne's)
2. Whose camera is on the chair? (Joseph's)
3. Whose chair is on the left? (Nadia's)
4. Whose suitcase is over there? (Tom's)
5. Whose postcards are those? (Carla's and Roberto's)
6. Whose car is that? (our neighbours')
7. Whose friends are they? (Yumi's and Anne's)
8. Whose jacket is on the chair? (Max's)
9. Whose cups are on the table? (the tourists')
10. Whose English class is this? (our class's)

TEACHER'S BOX: In **whose** questions, the subject pronoun in the answer agrees in number with the object possessed, and the possessive pronoun agrees in number and gender with the possessor (owner) of the object:

Whose car is that?   **It's ours.**

Whose books are those?   **They're mine.**

Listening and Speaking: Using Idioms

I'm Looking for a Jacket

A. Practise the expressions with the teacher.

on sale	= **on special**
Do you have a (blue jacket)?	= **Does it come in** (blue)?
(response to "Thank you.")	= **You're welcome.**

a hardware store   a furniture store   a clothing store

B. Listen and answer the questions.

  1. What is Nadia looking for?
  2. What colour does Nadia want?

C. Listen and write the words.

Sales clerk: Can I help you?

Nadia: Yes. I'm looking for a jacket.

Sales clerk: These jackets are _____ special. We're having a sale.

Nadia: Oh, I like this one. Does it come _____ blue?

Sales clerk: No, it only _____ in black.

Nadia: Well, thanks anyway.

Sales Clerk: You_____ welcome.

D. Practise the conversation with a partner.

What Are You Doing Today?

A. Practise the expressions with the teacher.

What are you doing?	= **What's up?**
at this moment	= **right now**
we can meet	= **we can get together**
It is a good idea.	= **It sounds good.**

B. Listen and answer the questions.

  1. What is Lili doing today?
  2. What is Yumi doing today?

a hairdresser   a bakery   a toy store   a video store   a laundromat

C. Listen and write the words.

> **Yumi:** Hi Lili. _____ up? Are you busy today?
>
> **Lili:** A little bit. I'm cleaning my house. How about you?
>
> **Yumi:** Oh, I'm relaxing today. _____ now I'm drinking coffee and reading the newspaper.
>
> **Lili:** Maybe we can _____ together later.
>
> **Yumi:** Sure. That _____ good. I'll call you later.
>
> **Lili:** 'Bye.

D. Practise the conversation with a partner.

Suggestions:

Work with a partner. Write a conversation. Begin with "What are you doing today?"

Act out your conversation for the class.

Ten-Minute Grammar Games

Charades

Focus: Practise present continuous form.

1. The class divides in half.
2. Students in each group write a sentence in present continuous form on a piece of paper.
    He is washing the dishes.
3. Group A gives the sentence to a student in Group B. The student acts out the sentence for his or her group. The students in Group B have a time limit (about 30 seconds) to guess the action. They get one point if they guess correctly within the time limit.
4. A student from Group A gets a sentence from Group B and acts it out for Group A in the same way.

The group with more correct answers wins.

Memory

Focus: Practise present continuous form. Review clothing items.

1. Students have one minute to look around the room and try to remember who is wearing what. They cannot write anything down.
2. The teacher calls on one student to volunteer to begin. The student comes to the front of the room and sits with his or her back to the class. Students take turns asking questions such as, "Who is wearing jeans today?"
    The student has to name only one person: "Kevin is wearing jeans today." If the student answers the question correctly, he or she gets one point.
3. The class continues asking questions about different articles of clothing, until the student makes a mistake or can't remember. Then another student goes to the front of the room to play.

I Spy

Focus: Practise the present continuous form.

1. The teacher reviews the meaning of "I spy."
2. The teacher begins by saying: "I spy someone who is wearing a T-shirt." (It is best to begin with an item that more than one person is wearing, such as a T-shirt or jeans.)
3. Students ask, "Is it Stefan?", "Is it Julie?" Give short answers: "No it isn't." Students keep guessing until they get the answer.
4. The student who guesses first continues the game by taking a turn to "spy."

Test Yourself

In the Park

A. Look at the picture. Complete the sentences:

_____ (take pictures). **Ali is taking pictures.**

1. _____ (sleep) under a tree.
2. _____ (write) a letter.
3. _____ (listen) to music.
4. _____ (read) a newspaper.
5. _____ (swim) in the lake.
6. _____ (play) soccer.

B. Write negative sentences. Use contractions.

1. The tourists are drinking coffee in the cafe.
2. The taxi is stopping outside the hotel.
3. They are listening to music.
4. We are waiting at the bus stop.
5. It is raining very hard today.
6. The people are watching a movie on TV.
7. I am looking for a telephone.
8. He is walking to the bus stop.
9. She is carrying a suitcase.
10. They are taking pictures of their friends.

C. Write **am**, **is**, or **are**.

1. _____ the tourists waiting in line?
2. _____ Ali buying jeans?
3. _____ they talking about their families?
4. _____ I waiting in the right place for a taxi?
5. _____ you enjoying your visit?
6. _____ Anne working this weekend?
7. _____ Max wearing a new T-shirt?
8. _____ Roberto having a good time?
9. _____ you using the telephone?
10. _____ we looking at the camera?

Find the Owner

A. Write the sentences with possessive pronouns:

This suitcase is Yumi's.   This suitcase is **hers**.

1. This camera is Chen's.
2. These sunglasses are Nadia's.
3. This car is Roberto's.
4. These keys are my keys.
5. These apples are for you and me.
6. This umbrella is Ali's.
7. This apartment is Max's.
8. These postcards are Tom's.
9. This wallet is Anne's.
10. This chair is Lili's.

B. Use possessive pronouns to answer the questions:

Whose room is this? (Max's)   **It's his.**

1. Whose friends are they? (Yumi's)
2. Whose car is that? (Tom's)
3. Whose guitar is near the couch? (Roberto's)
4. Whose brothers are in the picture? (Chen's)
5. Whose umbrella is on the floor? (Nadia's)
6. Whose coffee cups are on the table? (yours)
7. Whose dictionary is on the chair? (Ali's)
8. Whose keys are in the door? (Anne's)
9. Whose dessert is in the kitchen? (Carla)
10. Whose camera is that? (Tom's)

13

Past Continuous Aspect: Affirmative, Negative, Question Form

Adverbs of Manner

Question Words "How" and "Why"

Object Pronouns

Affirmative

I was	
you were	
he was	
she was	
it was	watching
we were	
you were	
they were	

Negative

I was not	
you were not	
he was not	
she was not	
it was not	watching
we were not	
you were not	
they were not	

Contraction

I wasn't	
you weren't	
he wasn't	
she wasn't	
it wasn't	watching
we weren't	
you weren't	
they weren't	

Question

was I	
were you	
was he	
was she	
was it	watching?
were we	
were you	
were they	

Words You Need

Match the pictures to the words.

1. quick, rapid, fast / slow
2. happy / sad
3. quiet / loud
4. early / late
5. easy / hard
6. lucky / unlucky
7. clear / unclear
8. sudden
9. careful / careless
10. angry
11. hungry

Understanding Grammar

UNDERSTAND: **Past Continuous Aspect**

Use the past continuous for past actions that were temporary:

> It **was raining** hard yesterday morning.

> Yumi **was wearing** a raincoat.

Use the verb **be** in the past tense before the **ing** form of the verb. The auxiliary verb shows time, negation, and person (singular or plural). The main verb with **ing** shows continuous aspect.

There is no contraction of the affirmative past continuous form. Put **not** after the auxiliary verb **be** to form a negative sentence in the past continuous:

> It **wasn't raining** yesterday.

> People **weren't carrying** umbrellas.

Affirmative		**Negative**	
I was		I was not	
you were		you were not	
he was		he was not	
she was		she was not	
it was	watching	it was not	watching
we were		we were not	
you were		you were not	
they were		they were not	

Contraction		**Question**	
I wasn't		was I	
you weren't		were you	
he wasn't		was he	
she wasn't		was she	
it wasn't	watching	was it	watching?
we weren't		were we	
you weren't		were you	
they weren't		were they	

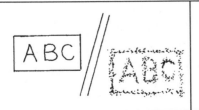

clear   unclear

careful

careless

sudden

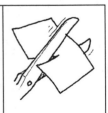

to cut

A. Look at the picture. Write the names of the people who were doing these things yesterday afternoon:

Yumi was wearing a raincoat.

1. wearing a raincoat
2. carrying an umbrella
3. taking a taxi
4. wearing a hat
5. waiting for a bus

6. carrying a suitcase
7. holding a newspaper
8. running to the hotel
9. sitting in a cafe
10. talking to the server

quiet   loud   to wave   to bite   to smell   to touch

B. Write the sentences in the negative:

It was snowing in Madrid.   **It wasn't snowing in Madrid.**

1. Tom was asking for directions.
2. Anne was carrying a newspaper.
3. Yumi was wearing her raincoat.
4. Ali and Chen were going to the bank.
5. We were sitting in the bus.
6. Lili was speaking to me.
7. Max was waiting for us at the hotel.
8. Roberto was looking for Nadia.
9. They were staying in an old hotel.
10. Nadia was studying Spanish.

UNDERSTAND: **Adverbs of Manner**

Adverbs of manner tell **how** actions happen. Put an adverb of manner after the main verb:

A turtle moves slowly.
A cheetah runs fast.
A cat walks quietly.
A lion roars loudly.

Common Adverbs of Manner

Regular Form (add **ly**)	
bad	badly
careful	carefully
clear	clearly
loud	loudly
nice	nicely
quick	quickly
quiet	quietly
rapid	rapidly
sad	sadly
slow	slowly
sudden	suddenly

Regular Form (change **y** to **i** and add **ly**)	
angry	angrily
easy	easily
happy	happily
hungry	hungrily
lucky	luckily
sad	sadly

Irregular Form	
early	early
fast	fast
good	well
hard	hard
late	late

TEACHER'S BOX: Adverbs of manner often end in **ly**. However, not all words that end in **ly** are adverbs of manner (lately, highly, hardly). For adverbs that end in **y**, apply the spelling rule, change the **y** to **i** and add **ly**:

happy / **happily**, easy / **easily**.

| a turtle | a cheetah | a lion | to roar | a newspaper | to give directions |

A. Write the adverbs. Put them in the crossword puzzle.

Across	Down
1. late	1. loud
3. sudden	2. clear
4. fast	5. easy
6. happy	7. angry
10. quiet	8. quick
11. hard	9. well
12. slow	

B. Which word is correct?

1. Anne was having a _____ (quiet/quietly) sleep.
2. The bus was moving _____ (slow/slowly).
3. They were playing music _____ (loud/loudly) at the party.
4. Max was playing tennis _____ (bad/badly) yesterday.
5. Please be _____ (quiet/quietly). I'm reading.
6. It was raining _____ (hard/hardly) this morning.
7. I can speak English _____ (good/well) now.
8. Lili was smiling _____ (nice/nicely).
9. The bus left _____ (late/lately) this morning.
10. It was a _____ (good/well) supper.

hard   soft   to move   to push   to pull   to knock

UNDERSTAND: **Question Words "How" and "Why"**

Use **how** to ask questions about manner (about **how** an action happened). Put **how** before the auxiliary verb. Put the subject after the auxiliary verb and before the main verb:

    How was he driving the car?   Slowly.

A. Choose the best answer.

    1. How was the teacher speaking? **hungrily suddenly clearly**
    2. How were they playing their music? **loudly luckily clearly**
    3. How was Anne smiling? **luckily happily loudly**
    4. How was the person sleeping? **quietly hungrily fast**
    5. How were the tourists listening? **carefully nicely loudly**
    6. How was it raining? **hard well nervously**
    7. How was the tour bus moving? **good fast nice**
    8. How were Max and Joseph eating? **badly hungrily sleepily**

Use **why** to ask questions about cause (the reason an action happened). Put **why** before the auxiliary verb. Put the subject after the auxiliary verb and before the main verb. The answer to a **why** question usually has the word **because**:

    Why was he driving fast? **because** he was late for work.

B. Match the questions and answers.

    1. Why was Max walking quickly?   a) because he was tired
    2. Why were Chen and Lili smiling?   b) because he was angry
    3. Why was Tom shouting?   c) because they missed the bus
    4. Why was Joseph making a sandwich? d) because they were happy
    5. Why were Nadia and Carla late?   e) because he was late
    6. Why were they drinking water?   f) because she was sad
    7. Why was Roberto sleeping?   g) because they were thirsty
    8. Why was Yumi crying?   h) because he was hungry

to play music   to sleep   to shout   to bleed   to ski   to skate

C.   Read about the robbery. Answer the questions.

Hotel Robbery!

Last night a robber came to the hotel. He waited patiently in the lobby. At 3:00 a.m., he went quietly up the stairs. He listened carefully at a door. A person was snoring loudly. The robber used a special key and opened the door easily. He entered the room slowly. After a minute, he found a wallet. He put the wallet quickly into his pocket. Then he left the room and walked rapidly down the stairs. He got into his car and drove away from the hotel. He was smiling happily.

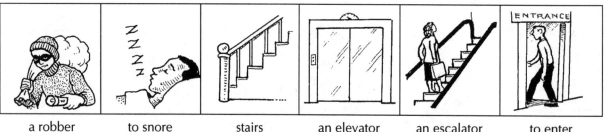

a robber   to snore   stairs   an elevator   an escalator   to enter

1. What time did the robber go upstairs?
2. How did he go upstairs?
3. Where did he listen?
4. What did he hear?
5. What did he use to enter the room?

6. What did he find in the room?
7. Where did he put the wallet?
8. How did he go away from the hotel?
9. What was he doing as he drove off?

D. Tell your partner the story.

UNDERSTAND: **Object Pronouns**

Use object pronouns to replace nouns as objects. Use object pronouns after verbs:
    We saw (a movie) **it.**

Use object pronouns after prepositions:
    We looked at (the people) **them.**

Subject Pronouns	Object Pronouns
I	me
you	you
he	him
she	her
it	it
we	us
you	you
they	them

> **TEACHER'S BOX:** English pronouns do not follow a consistent pattern: **you - you, it - it,** but **I - me, he - him, she - her, we - us, they - them.** This inconsistency can be difficult for students to master.

A. Choose the correct pronoun.

1. Ali showed _____ (he/him) his camera.
2. Her friend sent a postcard to _____ (she/her).
3. _____ (They/Them) came here from Hong Kong.
4. Anne went to the movie with _____ (I/me) yesterday.
5. Roberto took a picture of _____ (they/them).
6. They met _____ (we/us) at the airport.
7. _____ (I/Me) got up early yesterday morning.
8. Tom and _____ (I/me) went to the party last night.
9. _____ (We/Us) left the party before Max.
10. They made dinner for _____ (we/us) last night.

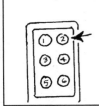    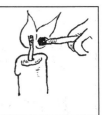

a button   a flashlight   a battery   a match   a matchbook   to light

B. Write the pronouns:

They knew **it** (my name).

1. Our teacher spoke to _____ (the students) in English.
2. _____ (Lili and Carla) went to a movie last night.
3. He often took _____ (his guitar) to parties.
4. _____ (The bus) arrived on time.
5. Roberto knew _____ (their names).
6. She often sent postcards to _____ (her sister).
7. Anne took a picture of _____ (my sister and me).
8. _____ (Ali and Nadia) gave a picture to Yumi.
9. They gave their telephone number to _____ (Max).
10. She spoke _____ (English) well.

Listening and Speaking: Using Idioms

What Were You Doing Yesterday?

A. Practise the expressions with the teacher.

nothing important	= **not much**
no	= **not really**
I really like (it).	= **I love (it).**

B. Listen and answer the questions.

1. Where was Yumi yesterday?
2. What was Yumi doing?
3. What was Yumi watching?

C. Listen and write the words.

Carla: Where were you yesterday?

Yumi: I was at home.

Carla: _____ were you doing?

Yumi: _____ much. I was watching TV.

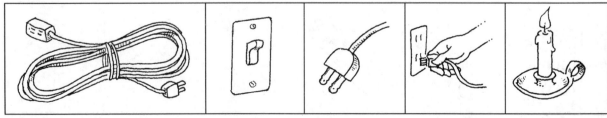

an extension cord   a switch   a plug   to plug in   a candle

Carla: Was there anything good on TV?

Yumi: _____ really. I was watching old movies.

Carla: I _____ old movies.

Yumi: Me too.

D. Practise the conversation with a partner.

How Was the Party?

A. Practise the expressions with the teacher.

Did you enjoy it?	= **How was it?**
not interesting	= **pretty boring**
Why?	= **How come?**
I'm sorry about that.	= **That's too bad.**

B. Listen and answer the questions.

1. Where was Joseph last night?
2. Why was the party boring?

C. Listen and write the words.

Tom: Where were you last night?

Joseph: I was at _____ party.

Tom: _____ was it?

Joseph: Pretty boring.

Tom: How _____?

Joseph: No one was dancing. No one was talking. I left early.

Tom: Oh, that's too _____.

D. Practise the conversation with a partner.

Suggestions:

Work with a partner. Write a conversation. Begin with "What were you doing last night?"
Act out your conversation for the class.

| to dance | guests | hosts | to introduce | refreshments | an invitation |

Ten-Minute Grammar Games

Charades

Focus: Practise adverbs of manner.

1. The class is divided in half.
2. Students in each group write a sentence with an adverb of manner on a piece of paper:

   He is eating slowly.
3. Group A gives the sentence to a student in Group B. The student acts out the sentence for his or her group. The students in Group B have a time limit (about 30 seconds) to guess the action and the adverb. They get one point if they guess correctly within the time limit.
4. A student from Group A gets a sentence from Group B and acts it out for Group A in the same way.

The group with more correct answers wins.

What's the Reason?

Focus: Practise asking and answering questions with **why** and **because**.

Students will be interested to note that these phrases are very useful when giving excuses!

1. The class brainstorms a list of questions beginning with "Why":

   "Why did you eat in a restaurant yesterday?" "Why did you stay home yesterday?"
2. Students work in groups. They are given a time limit, and asked to come up with as many answers as they can, beginning with "because." The group with the most suggestions, or with the most creative suggestions, wins.

Test Yourself

Then and Now

Use the past continuous form of the verb.

1. Anne is living in Montreal now. Last year she _____ in Chicago.
2. We are speaking English now. Yesterday we _____ Spanish.
3. Nadia and Ali are watching the news on TV. Last night they _____ a movie.
4. Our friends are travelling in Italy this summer. Last summer they _____ in England.
5. Today it is raining. Yesterday it _____ (snow).
6. This weekend Tom is visiting his friends. Last weekend his friends _____ him.
7. I am feeling happy today. Yesterday I _____ sad.
8. Yumi is playing tennis this afternoon. This morning she _____ her homework.

9. Joseph is resting in his room today. Yesterday _____ pictures of his friends.
10. Max's friends are living in Miami now. Last year they _____ in Toronto.

Anne's Story

In 1990, Anne was studying at McGill University. She was studying medicine. She was a good student and she learned quickly. Anne also studied very hard. On the weekends she worked in a drug store. She worked because she needed money to pay for her studies.

Answer the questions.

1. When was Anne studying at university?
2. Where was Anne studying?
3. What was she studying?
4. How did she study?
5. Where did she work on the weekends?
6. Why did she work on the weekends?

Vocabulary

Find the opposites:

happy   sad

1.	fast	a)	tall
2.	quiet	b)	hard
3.	good	c)	first
4.	short	d)	slow
5.	late	e)	bad
6.	last	f)	loud
7.	easy	g)	early
8.	thin	h)	fat

Adverbs

Choose the correct adverb.

1. We were walking _____ (quick/quickly).
2. It was raining _____ (hard/hardly).
3. They were playing music _____ (loudly/loud).
4. Their airplane left _____ (late/lately).
5. The cheetah was running _____ (fast/fastly).
6. We were talking _____ (quiet/quietly).
7. He was smiling _____ (happy/happily).
8. She was looking at the dessert _____ (hungry/hungrily).
9. They were looking around _____ (careful/carefully).
10. They were moving _____ (quick/quickly).

176

Object Pronouns

Complete the sentences with the correct pronouns.

1. Chen gave the keys to _____. (Tom)
2. Lili smiled at _____. (Nadia)
3. Max ate dinner with _____. (his friends)
4. Yumi had a present for _____. (you and me)
5. Roberto was looking at _____. (Carla)
6. Anne took a picture of _____. (Lili and Chen)
7. Lili wrote a letter to _____. (her sister)
8. Tom bought his car from _____. (his brother)
9. Max gave a magazine to _____. (Joseph)
10. Carla wrote a letter to _____. (her friends)

14

"Will" for Future Time: Affirmative, Negative, Question Form

"Be going to" for Future Plans: Affirmative, Negative, Question Form

Expressions of Future Time

Prepositions of Direction and Position "to," "at"

"Will" Affirmative	
I will	
you will	
he will	
she will	
it will	stay
we will	
you will	
they will	

Contraction	
I'll	
you'll	
he'll	
she'll	
it'll	stay
we'll	
you'll	
they'll	

Question	
will I	
will you	
will he	
will she	
will it	stay?
will we	
will you	
will they	

Negative	
I will not	
you will not	
he will not	
she will not	
it will not	stay
we will not	
you will not	
they will not	

Contraction	
I won't	
you won't	
he won't	
she won't	
it won't	stay
we won't	
you won't	
they won't	

"Be Going To" Affirmative
I am going to
you are going to
he is going to
she is going to
it is going to
we are going to
you are going to
they are going to

walk

Contraction
I'm going to
you're going to
he's going to
she's going to
it's going to
we're going to
you're going to
they're going to

walk

Negative
I am not going to
you are not going to
he is not going to
she is not going to
it is not going to
we are not going to
you are not going to
they are not going to

walk

Contraction
I'm not going to
you aren't going to
he isn't going to
she isn't going to
it isn't going to
we aren't going to
you aren't going to
they aren't going to

walk

Question
am I going to
are you going to
is he going to
is she going to
is it going to
are we going to
are you going to
are they going to

walk?

Understanding Grammar

UNDERSTAND: **"Will" for Future Time**

Use **will** to:	
make promises about the future	I **will help** you on Friday.
to show willingness to do something	I **will answer** the door.
to predict the future	He **will pass** the exam.

| to promise | to predict | to pass | Thanksgiving | Halloween | Easter |

Put the auxiliary verb **will** before the main verb. Use the base form of the main verb. The contraction of **will** is **'ll** (e.g., **I'll**):

It **will** snow in November.   It**'ll snow** in November.

"Will" Affirmative		Contraction	
I will		I'll	
you will		you'll	
he will		he'll	
she will		she'll	
it will	stay	it'll	stay
we will		we'll	
you will		you'll	
they will		they'll	

Language in Transition

In the past, the affirmative form of **will** in the first person was **shall**. Today, it is more common to say **I will**, **we will**. **Shall** is used in some formulaic questions such as, "Shall I open the window?" "Shall we eat?"

A.   Write these sentences in future time. Use **will**:

She plays the piano for us. She **will** play the piano for us.

1.   It snows in Toronto in January.
2.   I visit my parents at Thanksgiving.
3.   She eats dinner at 8:00.
4.   It is on TV at six o'clock.
5.   They eat dinner in a restaurant.
6.   We go to the beach in the morning.
7.   I am here for the English exam.
8.   He comes home at six o'clock.
9.   They take a walk near the beach.
10.   You watch the news on TV.

Christmas   New Year's   Mother's Day/Father's Day   Valentine's Day

B. Choose the correct verb. Use each verb once. Use the contraction with will.

be   bring   cook   help   play   tell   call   say   talk   meet   come

Anne: It will be hot this weekend. What do you think about a picnic?

Yumi: That's a great idea. I'll _____ you plan it.

Anne: Good. I _____ to you this evening to make plans.

Yumi: Okay. I _____ home after six o'clock.

Anne: What about Roberto and Carla?

Yumi: They love picnics. They _____ yes.

Anne: Max likes picnics. He _____ for sure.

Yumi: Nadia is a good cook. Maybe she _____ some food.

Anne: Chen and Joseph always enjoy soccer. They _____ a soccer ball.

Yumi: I _____ Tom about the picnic too.

Anne: Great. He _____ his guitar.

Yumi: Let's have the picnic at noon. We _____ at the park

Anne: Yes. I _____ you tonight to talk about the food.

a picnic   a lake   a park   a tree   a flower   clouds

UNDERSTAND: **"Will" for Future Time, Question Form**

Put **will** before the subject. Use a question mark (**?**) at the end of the sentence:

Will you be there on Tuesday?

Question	
will I	
will you	
will he	
will she	
will it	stay?
will we	
will you	
will they	

A. Make questions with the sentences. Use **will**:

It will be sunny tomorrow.   **Will** it **be** sunny tomorrow?

1. Tom and Ali will be here soon.
2. Anne will go back to work next week.
3. You will help me find my glasses.
4. He will telephone you tomorrow.
5. She will carry it for you.
6. Roberto will send us copies of the picture.
7. The car will start in cold weather.
8. Nadia and Carla will choose the restaurant.
9. Max will study English in Florida.
10. The bus will take us to the airport.

B. Match the statement and the question:

I'll finish at five o'clock.   Will you wait for me?

1. I'll visit you at seven.
2. This suitcase is heavy.
3. I didn't hear the weather report.
4. There will be an exam tomorrow.
5. We need some music.
6. The phone is ringing.
7. It's a formal party.
8. We need some dessert.
9. I can't find my glasses.
10. You have a good camera.

a) Will it be difficult?
b) Will you be home?
c) Will you bring your guitar?
d) Will you make a cake?
e) Will you answer it, please?
f) Will you take our pictures?
g) Will it be sunny tomorrow?
h) Will you help me look for them?
i) Will you help me carry it?
j) Will you wear your new dress?

a copy   noon   a sunny day   to ring   a party

UNDERSTAND: **"Will" for Future Time Negative**

Use **not** after **will** to make a sentence negative. The contraction of **will not** is **won't**:

I **will not be** at home.   I **won't be** at home.

Negative	
I will not	
you will not	
he will not	
she will not	
it will not	stay
we will not	
you will not	
they will not	

Contraction	
I won't	
you won't	
he won't	
she won't	
it won't	stay
we won't	
you won't	
they won't	

A. Write these sentences in the negative. Use **won't**:

She will tell us her mark.   She **won't tell** us her mark.

1. He will pass the exam.
2. That bus will leave on time.
3. He will call his friend tomorrow.
4. They will tell us about it.
5. I will go out in the rain.
6. She will remember to phone tonight.
7. You will be cold with that coat.
8. We will be home tonight.
9. The train will arrive on time.
10. It will rain on the weekend.

B. Read and answer the questions. Answer "Yes, (it, there, they) will" or "No, (it, there, they) won't."

The weatherman says that temperatures will go down to −18° later tonight. He predicts that twenty-five centimetres of snow will fall by tomorrow morning. Workers will begin to clear snow during the night. They probably won't finish before tomorrow afternoon. It will be hard to walk on the sidewalks. Cars won't start easily. Many people won't arrive at work on time. Late tomorrow afternoon temperatures will go up. There won't be snow on the streets or sidewalks. The city will be back to normal.

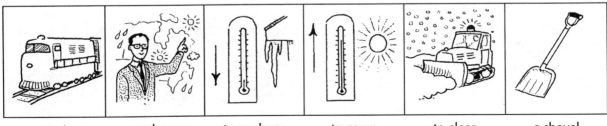

a train   a weatherman   to go down   to go up   to clear   a shovel

1. Will it be cold later tonight?
2. Will temperatures be below zero?
3. Will snow fall?
4. Will workers start clearing snow in the morning?
5. Will they finish clearing snow at noon tomorrow?
6. Will it be easy to walk on the sidewalks?
7. Will cars start easily?
8. Will people be late for work?
9. Will temperatures stay down all day?
10. Will the city be back to normal at the end of the day?

UNDERSTAND: **"Be Going To" for Future Plans**

Use **be going to** for:	
decisions or plans for the future	We are going to visit France this summer.
intentions for the immediate future	I'm going to go to bed early tonight.
things we expect to happen immediately	I think that picture is going to fall.

Put the auxiliary verb phrase **be going to** before the main verb. Use the base form of the main verb:

They **are going to** visit Japan next summer.

"Be Going To" Affirmative

I am going to
you are going to
he is going to
she is going to
it is going to   walk

we are going to
you are going to
they are going to

TEACHER'S BOX: These exercises do not contrast the use of **will** and **be going to**. They focus on the form, and use appropriate examples of the two structures separately.

a stop sign   traffic lights   a crosswalk   a parking lot   a parking meter   school zone

A. Write sentences about the future. Use **be going to**:

I usually watch the news at six o'clock. **I'm going to** watch the news at six o'clock.

1. Anne goes to bed at 11 o'clock.
2. Roberto takes a taxi on Mondays.
3. They go to movies on the weekend.
4. We watch the news on TV.
5. Max is late for work today.
6. I go to bed early on Sunday nights.
7. The store closes at five o'clock today.
8. Nadia and Yumi play tennis near the hotel.
9. Joseph asks the tour guide for information.
10. Tom and Ali take pictures of the group.

B. Which sentences are wrong? Correct wrong verb phrases:

They are going rest after dinner.   They are going **to** rest after dinner.

1. I am going go home early today.
2. We are going to eat at seven o'clock.
3. Yumi is going play tennis this afternoon.
4. Anne is going to go to the dentist.
5. They are go to buy stamps at the post office.
6. Tom is going to send postcards to his friends.
7. Lili and Carla are going to shop downtown today.
8. Roberto is going wait on the bench.
9. I am go to eat lunch in a restaurant.
10. It is going rain this afternoon.

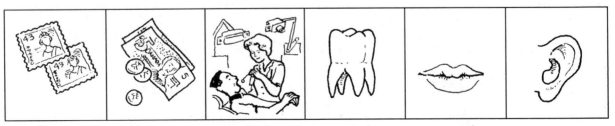

| stamps | money | a dentist | a tooth | a mouth | an ear |

UNDERSTAND: **"Be Going To" Negative**

Put **not** after the verb **be**. There are two forms of the negative contraction: **He's not going to** or **He isn't going to**; **They're not going to** or **They aren't going to**.

It **isn't going to** rain today.

Negative	**Contraction Form A**	**Contraction Form B**
I am not going to you are not going to he is not going to she is not going to it is not going to walk we are not going to you are not going to they are not going to	I'm not going to you aren't going to he isn't going to she isn't going to it isn't going to walk we aren't going to you aren't going to they aren't going to	I'm not going to you're not going to he's not going to she's not going to it's not going to walk we're not going to you're not going to they're not going to

A. Write the sentences in the negative. Use Contraction Form A.

It is going to snow. It **isn't going to** snow.

1. They are going to meet us downstairs.
2. You are going to watch TV.
3. She is going to forget her purse.
4. I am going to tell him.
5. We are going to stay in this hotel.
6. They are going to play tennis today.
7. He is going to eat an orange.
8. You are going to need an umbrella.
9. I am going to stay up late.
10. She is going to cook dinner tonight.

B. Complete the verb phrases:

You are **not** going to need an umbrella.

1. We are _____ going to watch TV this evening.
2. You are not _____ to need a coat today.
3. Anne _____ not going to get up early.
4. Chen and Lili are not going _____ have breakfast.
5. Tom is _____ going to go to the party.
6. I _____ not going to take any money with me.

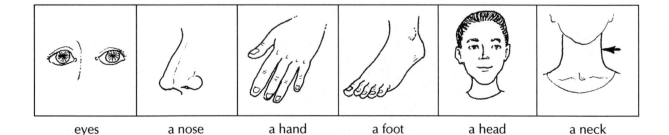

| eyes | a nose | a hand | a foot | a head | a neck |

7. Carla is not _____ to wait for the bus.
8. You are not going _____ carry that box alone.
9. Nadia and Ali are _____ going to come on the tour.
10. Max is not going _____ meet us in the lobby.

UNDERSTAND: **"Be Going To" Question Form**

Put the auxiliary verb **be** before the subject to form a question with **be going to**:

Are you **going to** take any pictures on the trip?

Question	
am I going to	
are you going to	
is he going to	
is she going to	
is it going to	walk?
are we going to	
are you going to	
are they going to	

A. Make questions with these sentences:

You are going to watch TV. **Are** you **going to** watch TV?

1. Tom is going to go downtown.
2. Yumi and Carla are going to meet later.
3. It is going to rain tonight.
4. We are going to enjoy that movie.
5. Roberto is going to take the bus.
6. They are going to take a taxi.
7. Anne is going to buy stamps.
8. Chen is going to drive there.
9. Max and Ali are going to drink coffee.
10. Nadia is going to phone you later.

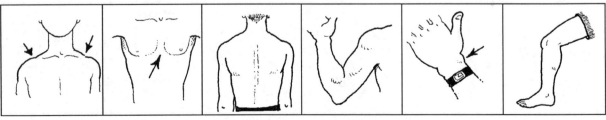

shoulders   a chest   a back   an arm   a wrist   a leg

B. Match questions and answers.

1. Where are we going to eat?
2. How are we going to get there?
3. Who is going to drive?
4. What are you going to wear?
5. What time are we going to go?
6. Where are we going to meet?
7. Why are we going to go to a restaurant?

a) at 7:00
b) in a restaurant
c) jeans and a shirt
d) because it is Joseph's birthday
e) in the lobby
f) by car
g) Joseph is

UNDERSTAND: **Expressions of Future Time**

Match the dates to the expressions of time.

		JANUARY 1995				
SUN	MON	TUES	WED	THURS	FRI	SAT
1	②	3	4	5	6	7
8	9	10	11	12	13	14
15	16	17	18	19	20	21
22	23	24	25	26	27	28
29	30					

Now: 10 a.m., Monday, January 2, 1995

1. Tuesday, January 3, 1995
2. 3 p.m., Monday, January 2, 1995
3. January 9-13, 1995
4. February 1995
5. January 1996
6. 8 p.m., Monday, January 2, 1995
7. 3 p.m., Tuesday, January 3, 1995

a) tomorrow
b) next year
c) next week
d) this evening
e) next month
f) tomorrow afternoon
g) this afternoon

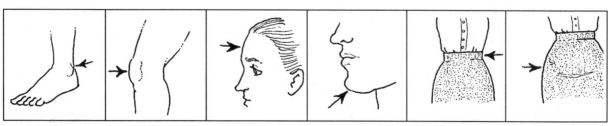

an ankle   a knee   a forehead   a chin   a waist   hips

UNDERSTAND: **Prepositions of Direction and Position**

Preposition "To"

Use the preposition **to** for direction. It tells where you are going. You use it with verbs that suggest movement (**go to, travel to, fly to, walk to**):

> **go to** the bank
> **drive to** the airport
> **walk to** school

Some expressions of place (**downtown, home, inside, outside, there**) don't use **to**:

> ✗ He went to home.
> ✔ He went home.

Preposition "At"

Use the preposition **at** for position. It tells where you are now:

> at the bank, at the airport, at school

Some expressions of place (downtown, inside, outside, there) don't use **at**:

> ✗ He is at downtown.
> ✔ He is downtown.

Use **to**, **at**, or **Ø** in the sentences.

1. Yumi and Anne will walk _____ downtown.
2. Max is going to study _____ home.
3. They are going to go _____ the airport to meet him.
4. Carla is going to go _____ the store with Lili.
5. We will wait _____ home for the phone call.
6. I am going to go _____ my English class this afternoon.
7. Let's go _____ there tomorrow morning.
8. He will wait for us _____ the bus stop.
9. Roberto and Nadia will go _____ the bank later.
10. The children are going to go _____ outside.

| outside | inside | downtown | a market | a train station | a bus stop |

Listening and Speaking: Using Idioms

What Are You Going to Do on the Weekend?

A. Practise the expressions with the teacher.

sleep late	= **sleep in**
no	= **nah**
relax, not work hard	= **take it easy**
Do you have any plans?	= **Any plans?**
I don't know.	= **Who knows?**

B. Listen and answer the questions.

1. What is Max going to do on Saturday morning?
2. Is Max going to play tennis on Saturday afternoon?
3. What is Tom going to do in the morning?

C. Listen and write the words.

Tom: What are you doing on the weekend?

Max: Well, on Saturday morning I'm going to sleep _____.

Tom: Are you going to play tennis Saturday afternoon?

Max: Nah. I'm going to take it _____ all day. How about you? _____ plans for Saturday?

Tom: I'm going to take my car to the garage in the morning. After that, _____ knows?

D. Practise the conversation with a partner.

to relax   to sleep in   to play cards   to collect stamps   to collect coins   to knit

This Is a Friend of Mine

A. Practise the expressions with the teacher.

come here	= **come on over**
my friend	= **a friend of mine**

B. Listen and answer the questions.

1. Who is Keiko?
2. Where is Keiko going to study English?

C. Listen and write the words.

Yumi: Tom, do you know my friend Keiko?

Tom: No, I don't. Can you introduce us?

Yumi: Sure. Come on _____. I_____ introduce you. Keiko, meet Tom. He's a friend of

_____.

Keiko: Nice to meet you, Tom.

Yumi: Tom, meet Keiko. She's going to study English in Vancouver.

Tom: _____ to meet you, Keiko.

D. Practise the conversation with a partner.

Suggestions

Work with a partner. Write a conversation. Begin with "What are you going to do on the weekend?"

Act out your conversation for the class.

Ten-Minute Grammar Games

Mystery Box

Focus: Practise **will** to predict future time.

1. The following time expressions are written on cards or pieces of paper:

next winter

next week

next September

next year

next weekend

next summer

in five years

2. The cards are placed in a box.

3. Each student picks a card and says a sentence about what he or she will do:
   Next summer **I'll be** in Toronto.

Chain

Focus: Practise **be going to** for discussing future plans.

This game can be played with the whole class or with smaller groups if the class is large.

1. The teacher begins with a sentence about future plans:
   On my vacation, **I'm going to** go to Spain.

2. The first student repeats and adds:
   On her vacation, **she's going to** go to Spain. On my vacation, **I'm going to** go to Mexico.

3. Students continue until someone breaks the chain by forgetting or making a grammatical error.

4. Someone begins a new chain.

Keep track of how long the class can sustain the chain. This game can be repeated at another time, either to review or to practise new structures. Each time, students try to beat their previous class record.

Test Yourself

Away From Home

Before Ali left his country he made some promises to his family. Write his promises with **will** or **won't**:

   study hard   **I will study hard.**

1. spend a lot of money
2. write home often
3. be sad
4. forget my old friends
5. make new friends

6. be happy
7. send postcards
8. wear warm clothes
9. eat good food
10. stay out late

Making Plans

Use the correct form of **be going to**.

1. Lili is tired from the tour. She _____ (relax) in her hotel room.
2. It is raining hard. Roberto _____ (take) a taxi to work.
3. Nadia lost her wallet on the subway. She _____ (go) to the police.
4. We are hungry but we don't have time. We _____ (eat) in a fast-food restaurant.

5. You want to see a popular singer. You _____ (buy) your tickets early.
6. Roberto is tired. He _____ (take) a holiday with his family.
7. Yumi is sick. She _____ (call) the doctor.
8. I don't like this hotel. I _____ (change) to a different hotel.
9. They need some food for dinner. They _____ (stop) at the supermarket on the way home.
10. Ali lost his umbrella. He _____ (buy) a new one at the department store.

Find the Errors

Correct the errors.

1. When are we go back to the hotel?
2. Who is going study this evening?
3. They not going to buy any fish today.
4. Is going to rain tomorrow?
5. I am go to walk on the beach after dinner.
6. What are you going ask the tour guide?
7. What time are the plane going to arrive?
8. Max not going to travel next year.
9. Where we going to meet this evening?
10. We are going not to see the new movie tonight.

Prepositions of Direction and Position

Choose the correct sentence:

✗ a) I am going at **downtown**.   ✔ b) I am going **downtown**.

1. a) I'm going to the airport.   b) I'm going at the airport.
2. a) She is to school.   b) She is at school.
3. a) He is sick at home.   b) He is sick at the home.
4. a) Max is walking at work.   b) Max is walking to work.
5. a) We are going New York.   b) We are going to New York.
6. a) They are waiting at the bus stop.   b) They are waiting to the bus stop.

15 | Review Unit

Count and Non-count Nouns

A. Use **some** or **any**.

1. She doesn't want _____ coffee.
2. He is waiting for _____ friends.
3. I am carrying _____ packages.
4. Do you have _____ apples?
5. We don't have _____ fish today.
6. Are you sending _____ postcards?
7. Do you have _____ stamps?
8. He is eating _____ cheese.
9. We can't find _____ sugar.
10. You don't need _____ milk in your coffee.

B. Use **there is** or **there are** in the affirmative, negative, or question form.

1. _____ some milk in the refrigerator.
2. _____ a holiday on Monday.
3. _____ any sugar on the table?
4. _____ some apples in the supermarket.
5. _____ some cups in the cupboard.
6. _____ a table in the kitchen.
7. _____ any water in the glasses?
8. _____ some rice in that pot on the stove.
9. _____ any salt in the sauce.
10. _____ any meat with the dinner?

193

Present Continuous

A. Look at the picture. Give the name of the person or thing:

It is arriving at the hotel.   **a bus**

1. They are sitting in a cafe.
2. He is reading the newspaper.
3. He is sitting on a bench.
4. She is buying postcards.
5. He is talking to a tour guide.

6. They are looking at some children.
7. He is taking pictures.
8. She is drinking coffee.
9. He is looking at a map.
10. She is drinking tea.

B. Answer the questions.

1. Who is wearing a jacket and shorts?
2. What is Roberto reading?
3. Where are the children standing?
4. What is Yumi drinking?
5. Who is sitting on the bench?

6. What is Tom looking at?
7. Who is wearing glasses?
8. Who is carrying an umbrella?
9. Who is wearing a hat?
10. Where is Carla drinking coffee?

C. Write the continuous form of these verbs:

walk   walking

1. sit
2. speak
3. carry
4. eat

5. take
6. play
7. buy
8. wear

9. plan
10. drink

D. Look at pictures of Friday night and Saturday night. Write six sentences about each picture.

E.   Work with a partner. Find six things that changed from Friday to Saturday:

On Friday night Chen was wearing a jacket.   On Saturday night Chen was wearing a sweater.

Past Continuous
Adverbs of Manner

A.   Write the adverb form of the word.

1.	bad	6.	sudden
2.	careful	7.	happy
3.	quick	8.	hard
4.	fast	9.	rapid
5.	slow	10.	easy

B.   Work with a partner. Read the story. Answer the questions.

A Car Accident

Last night Tom was coming home in a taxi. It was raining hard. The taxi was driving fast. Suddenly, there was an accident. Tom wasn't wearing his seat belt. He fell and hurt his arm badly. He went to the hospital in an ambulance.

Roberto and Chen went to the hospital. Tom was lying on a bed. Two nurses were asking him questions. He was waiting for the doctor. He wasn't looking happy because the doctor wasn't coming quickly. The nurses were giving him a shot.

1.	How was Tom coming home?	6.	Where was Tom lying?
2.	How was it raining?	7.	What were the nurses asking him?
3.	How was the taxi driving?	8.	Who was he waiting for?
4.	Why was Tom hurt in the accident?	9.	Why wasn't he looking happy?
5.	How did he go to hospital?	10.	What were the nurses giving him?

Future with "Be Going To"

A.   Read and answer the questions.

Tonight we are going to have a party for Yumi's birthday. Anne is going to bring a birthday cake. Lili and Carla are going to shop for a birthday present. Roberto and Max are going to play music. Yumi doesn't know about the party because her friends are going to surprise her.

Nadia and Ali aren't going to stay long because they don't want to be tired in the morning. Nadia's sister is going to arrive early tomorrow morning. Nadia and Ali are going to meet her at the airport. They are going to take a taxi to the airport. Nadia and Ali are going to go to sleep early tonight.

1.   What are Yumi's friends going to do?

2.   What is Anne going to do?

3. What are Lili and Carla going to shop for?
4. What are Roberto and Max going to do?
5. Why doesn't Yumi know about the party?
6. Why aren't Nadia and Ali going to stay long?
7. When is Nadia's sister going to arrive?
8. Where are Nadia and Ali going to meet Nadia's sister?
9. How are they going to go to the airport?
10. When are they going to go to sleep tonight?

B. Make questions:

We are going to arrive early. (when) **When are we going to arrive?**

1. We are going to go a party. (where)
2. Anne is going to bring a birthday cake. (what)
3. Lili and Carla are going to shop. (what)
4. Roberto and Max are going to play music. (what)
5. Yumi's friends are going to surprise her. (what)
6. Nadia and Ali aren't going to stay long. (who)
7. Nadia's sister is going to arrive tomorrow. (when)
8. They are going to meet her at the airport. (where)
9. They are going to go to bed early. (when)
10. They are going to use an alarm clock. (what)

Appendix 1

Letters of the Alphabet

Print

Aa Bb Cc Dd Ee Ff Gg Hh Ii Jj Kk Ll Mm Nn Oo Pp Qq Rr Ss Tt Uu Vv Ww Xx Yy Zz

Write

Aa Bb Cc Dd Ee Ff Gg Hh Ii Jj Kk Ll Mm Nn Oo Pp Qq Rr Ss Tt Uu Vv Ww Xx Yy Zz

Cardinal Numbers

1	one	21	twenty-one	41	forty-one	61	sixty-one	81	eighty-one
2	two	22	twenty-two	42	forty-two	62	sixty-two	82	eighty-two
3	three	23	twenty-three	43	forty-three	63	sixty-three	83	eighty-three
4	four	24	twenty-four	44	forty-four	64	sixty-four	84	eighty-four
5	five	25	twenty-five	45	forty-five	65	sixty-five	85	eighty-five
6	six	26	twenty-six	46	forty-six	66	sixty-six	86	eighty-six
7	seven	27	twenty-seven	47	forty-seven	67	sixty-seven	87	eighty-seven
8	eight	28	twenty-eight	48	forty-eight	68	sixty-eight	88	eighty-eight
9	nine	29	twenty-nine	49	forty-nine	69	sixty-nine	89	eighty-nine
10	ten	30	thirty	50	fifty	70	seventy	90	ninety
11	eleven	31	thirty-one	51	fifty-one	71	seventy-one	91	ninety-one
12	twelve	32	thirty-two	52	fifty-two	72	seventy-two	92	ninety-two
13	thirteen	33	thirty-three	53	fifty-three	73	seventy-three	93	ninety-three
14	fourteen	34	thirty-four	54	fifty-four	74	seventy-four	94	ninety-four
15	fifteen	35	thirty-five	55	fifty-five	75	seventy-five	95	ninety-five
16	sixteen	36	thirty-six	56	fifty-six	76	seventy-six	96	ninety-six
17	seventeen	37	thirty-seven	57	fifty-seven	77	seventy-seven	97	ninety-seven
18	eighteen	38	thirty-eight	58	fifty-eight	78	seventy-eight	98	ninety-eight
19	nineteen	39	thirty-nine	59	fifty-nine	79	seventy-nine	99	ninety-nine
20	twenty	40	forty	60	sixty	80	eighty	100	one hundred

Ordinal Numbers

1st	first	9th	ninth	17th	seventeenth	25th	twenty-fifth
2nd	second	10th	tenth	18th	eighteenth	26th	twenty-sixth
3rd	third	11th	eleventh	19th	nineteenth	27th	twenty-seventh
4th	fourth	12th	twelfth	20th	twentieth	28th	twenty-eighth
5th	fifth	13th	thirteenth	21st	twenty-first	29th	twenty-ninth
6th	sixth	14th	fourteenth	22nd	twenty-second	30th	thirtieth
7th	seventh	15th	fifteenth	23rd	twenty-third	31st	thirty-first
8th	eighth	16th	sixteenth	24th	twenty-fourth		

Colours

red
yellow
orange
green
blue
purple
brown
black
white
grey

Directions

north
west
east
south

Seasons

winter
spring
summer
winter

Continents

Africa
Asia
Australia
Europe
North America
South America

Countries and Nationalities

(20 largest countries by population)

China	Chinese	Mexico	Mexican
India	Indian	Vietnam	Vietnamese
United States	American	Philippines	Filipino
Indonesia	Indonesian	Germany	German
Brazil	Brazilian	Italy	Italian
Russia	Russian	United Kingdom	British
Pakistan	Pakistani	Turkey	Turkish
Japan	Japanese	France	French
Bangladesh	Bangladesh	Thailand	Thai
Nigeria	Nigeria	Iran	Iranian

National Holidays

New Year's Day	January 1	St. Jean-Baptiste Day	June 24th
Valentine's Day	February 14	Labour Day	1st Monday in September
Easter	March-April	Thanksgiving	2nd Monday in October
Mother's Day	2nd Sunday in May	Halloween	October 31
Father's Day	3rd Sunday in June	Remembrance Day	November 11
Victoria Day	3rd Monday in May	Christmas Day	December 25
Canada Day	July 1st		

Prepositions of Place

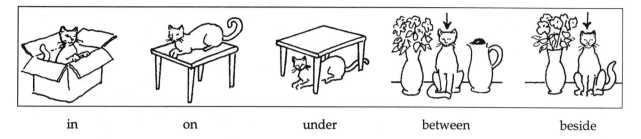

in   on   under   between   beside

Partitives

a piece of bread, cake
a loaf of bread
a can of tuna, soup
a box of crackers, tissues
a package of noodles, cookies
a slice of bread, cheese
a carton of milk, juice

Appendix 2

Time

It is nine o'clock.

It is nine fifteen.
It is a quarter past nine.

It is nine thirty
It is half past nine.

It is nine forty-five.
It is a quarter to ten.

Days of the Week

Monday	(Mon.)
Tuesday	(Tues.)
Wednesday	(Wed.)
Thursday	(Thurs.)
Friday	(Fri.)
Saturday	(Sat.)
Sunday	(Sun.)

Months of the Year

January	(Jan.)
February	(Feb.)
March	(Mar.)
April	(Apr.)
May	
June	
July	
August	(Aug.)
September	(Sept.)
October	(Oct.)
November	(Nov.)
December	(Dec.)

Adverbs of Time

Past	Present	Future
yesterday	today	tomorrow
yesterday morning	now	tomorrow morning
yesterday afternoon		tomorrow afternoon
yesterday evening		tomorrow evening
last night		tomorrow night
last Saturday		next Monday
last week		next week
last month		next month
last year		next year

Prepositions of Time

in July
in 1995

on March 15
on Tuesday

at three o'clock

Appendix 3

Common Wh-Questions and Answers

What is your name?	My name is _____. I'm _____.
Where are you from?	I'm from _____.
How old are you?	I'm _____.
What is your telephone number?	It's _____.
What is your address?	It's _____.
What is your job?	I'm a/an _____.
What language do you speak?	I speak _____.

Simple Aspect

I am, I am not, etc.
I was, I was not, etc.
I will be, I won't be, etc.

I have, I don't have
I had, I didn't have
I will have, I won't have

I work, I don't work
I worked, I didn't work
I will work, I won't work

Continuous Aspect

I am eating, I'm not eating
I was eating, I wasn't eating
I will be eating, I won't be eating

I am working, I am not working
I was working, I wasn't working
I will be working, I won't be working

Imperatives

Open the window.
Turn right.
Be careful.

"Let's" for Suggestions

Let's open the window.
Let's turn right.
Let's be careful.

Past Tense Irregular Verbs

become	became	leave	left
begin	began	lose	lost
bring	brought	make	made
build	built	pay	paid
buy	bought	put	put
come	came	read	read*
cost	cost	ride	rode
cut	cut	run	ran
drink	drank	see	saw
eat	ate	sell	sold
fall	fell	send	sent
feel	felt	sit	sat
find	found	sleep	slept
forget	forgot	speak	spoke
give	gave	take	took
go	went	teach	taught
get	got	tell	told
grow	grew	think	thought
have	had	understand	understood
hear	heard	wear	wore
know	knew		

*Note that the pronunciation changes in the past tense to "red."

Index

Test Yourself Answers

Unit 1

Meeting and Greeting (Page 11)

A.
1. a
2. a
3. a
4. b
5. a
6. b
7. a
8. a

B.
1. b
2. d
3. e
4. a
5. f
6. c

Verb "Be" (Page 12)

A.
1. are
2. is
3. am
4. are
5. are
6. is
7. is
8. are
9. is
10. are

B.
1. He's American.
2. We're from Spain.
3. I'm happy to meet you.
4. She's a child.
5. I'm 18 years old.
6. They're friends.
7. He's 26.
8. It's late.
9. We're tourists.
10. She's short.

Subject Pronouns (Page 13)

1. She
2. They
3. It
4. I
5. He
6. you
7. I
8. She
9. They
10. You

Vocabulary (Page 13)

A.
1. woman
2. job
3. Peru
4. friend
5. China

B.
1. women
2. friends
3. students
4. children
5. doctors
6. people
7. tourists
8. rooms
9. men
10. teachers

C.
1. name, from, last, old
2. meet, from, Where, Egyptian
3. going, bad, good

Unit 2

Short Answers (Page 26)

A.
1. No, he isn't.
2. No, he isn't.
3. No, he isn't.
4. Yes, he is.

B.
1. No, they aren't.
2. No, she isn't.
3. Yes, they are.
4. No, it isn't.
5. Yes, they are.

Question Form (Page 26)

1. What is your occupation?
2. What are your names?
3. Is it cold in San Diego?
4. Are people in Taiwan Chinese?
5. Is it rainy in Vancouver?

Negative Form (Page 27)

1. October and November aren't in summer. They're in fall.
2. April isn't in winter. It's in spring.
3. January isn't in spring. It's in winter.

4. July and August aren't in fall. They're in summer.
5. February isn't in summer. It's in winter.

Verb Review (Page 27)

A. How **are** you? How **is** the weather in Vancouver? **Is** the summer hot or cold? In Caracas, **it's** hot and sunny. **Are** you happy there? Is Pedro in your English class?

Thank you for your letter. I **am** fine. Pedro **is** fine too. We **are** in the same English class. He is very good at English. I **am** not good at English.

The weather here **is** not great, but today it is sunny and warm. I **am** happy in Vancouver. It **is** an interesting city.

B.
1. It is hot and sunny.
2. He is fine.
3. Yes, they are.
4. It is not great.
5. Yes, he is.

Vocabulary (Page 28)

1. winter
2. class
3. China
4. January
5. hot

Unit 3

Demonstrative Adjectives (Page 41)

1. These
2. That
3. This
4. These
5. Those

Verbs (Page 42)

A.
1. was
2. were
3. was
4. were
5. was
6. was
7. were
8. was
9. were
10. was

B.
1. They were in New York.
2. Yes, she was.
3. No, she wasn't.
4. No, she wasn't. Anne was a guide.
5. at restaurants, department stores, theatres
6. on Monday

Ask Questions (Page 42)

1. Was the weather good?
2. Was the movie good?
3. Were they hungry?
4. Was the food good?
5. Was the hotel new?

Vocabulary (Page 42)

1. airport
2. hungry
3. happy
4. building
5. picture
6. child

7. suitcase
8. weather
9. restaurant
10. movies
11. young
12. strong
13. tired
14. hotel
15. brother
16. yesterday
17. camera
18. bus
19. mother
20. good

Unit 4

Verbs (Page 55)

A.
1. can
2. can't
3. can
4. can
5. can't

B.
1. Can Joseph play tennis?
2. Can you speak French?
3. Can Nadia drive a car?
4. Can Max take good pictures?
5. Can Yumi cook spaghetti?

Possessive Adjectives (Page 55)

1. My
2. Their
3. Our
4. His
5. Your
6. Her

Indefinite Articles (Page 55)

1. an engineer
2. a piano
3. a camera
4. a suitcase
5. an apple
6. a child
7. a fork
8. a guitar
9. an animal
10. an orderly

Conversations (Page 56)

1. Can, can't, Can
2. Can, Can
3. Can, can

Vocabulary (Page 56)

1. e
2. g
3. h
4. i
5. j
6. a
7. f
8. c
9. d
10. b

Unit 6

Verb "Have" (Page 78)

A.
1. has
2. has
3. doesn't have
4. doesn't have
5. has
6. don't have
7. has
8. don't have
9. has
10. have

B.
1. Do, have
2. Do, have
3. doesn't have
4. has
5. Do, have
6. doesn't have
7. Does, have
8. doesn't have
9. Does, have any
10. Does, have

Possessive Nouns (Page 79)

1. Max's walkman is small.
2. The teacher's glasses are new.
3. Lili's sisters are young.
4. Yumi's friends are nice.
5. The bus driver's job is hard.
6. Tom's apartment is comfortable.
7. Carla's children are young.
8. Anne's brother is tall.
9. The climate in Vancouver is rainy.
10. Roberto's sunglasses are black.

Find the Errors (Page 79)

1. My room doesn't have **any** towels.
2. She **has** short hair.
3. We **don't have** any friends here/We have **some** friends here.
4. My sister **has** two children.
5. Correct
6. Our apartment has **big** rooms.
7. Correct
8. The apartment doesn't **have** furniture.
9. You **have** free time in the evening.
10. The tourist **has** a new camera.

Unit 7

Pablo Is from Columbia (Page 93)

A. 1. comes
2. lives
3. has
4. is
5. likes
6. visit
7. go (travel)
8. travel (go)
9. enjoy
10. sends

B. 1. He comes from Columbia.
2. He comes from Bogota.
3. He lives in Oshawa.
4. He is an engineer.
5. Yes, he does.
6. They visit Columbia.
7. They take their vacation in August.
8. Yes, they do.
9. Yes, they do.
10. He sends postcards.

Daily Routine (Page 94)

A. 1. Do you usually watch TV in the evening?
2. Does Lili always drive to work?
3. Do Carla and Roberto speak French?
4. Do her parents live in a small town?
5. Does Chen work downtown?
6. Do I watch TV in the afternoon?
7. Does Nadia write to her family?
8. Do Ali and Tom play tennis after work?
9. Do they drink tea in the afternoon?
10. Does Anne wake up early?

B. 1. Lili and her family don't live in China.
2. Tom doesn't leave for work late.
3. Tourists don't always eat in restaurants.
4. Roberto doesn't go to bed early.
5. We don't do homework every night.
6. Ali and Nadia don't watch TV often.
7. Chen doesn't cook dinner.
8. Max doesn't study very hard.
9. We don't go to the supermarket every day.
10. They don't understand Spanish.

Find the Errors (Page 94)

1. He **sometimes goes** to the beach.
2. Correct
3. It is **never cold** in Acapulco.
4. Correct
5. Hotels **always give** guests keys.
6. Correct
7. Young people **usually like** loud music.
8. Correct
9. Correct
10. The weather in Canada is **sometimes hot**.

Where Are They? (Page 95)

Possible answers:
1. The camera is on the table.
2. The pen is on the table.
3. The pen is beside the camera.
4. The umbrella is in the bag.
5. The book is under the table.
6. The suitcase is between the table and the door.
7. The bag is beside the table.

Vocabulary (Page 95)

1. juice
2. spring
3. beach
4. house
5. keys
6. tour
7. movies
8. always
9. late
10. rice

Unit 8

Joanna's Story (Page 109)

Joanna **studied** English at the University of British Columbia. She **liked** her class and she **worked** very hard. She **had** classes four days a week. She **didn't have** class on Fridays.

Joanna **loved** Vancouver and **enjoyed** different activities. Sometimes she **walked** on the beach. On Saturdays she usually **played** tennis. She **visited** friends and they **did** their homework together.

Find the Errors (Page 109)

1. Max **studied** hard for his exam.
2. The students **enjoyed** their English class.
3. Yumi **planned** a trip to Seattle.
4. Anne **did not like** the new restaurant.
5. The porter **carried** the suitcases to the room.
6. Correct

7. Correct
8. The guide **helped** the tourists.
9. Anne **cooked** rice for dinner last night.
10. We **didn't know** her name.

Max's Terrible Week (Page 110)
1. On Monday Max's alarm clock **rang**.
2. He **woke up** on time.
3. On Tuesday it **rained**.
4. Max **had** an umbrella.
5. Max **took** his lunch to work.
6. He **went** out on Friday night.
7. On Saturday he **got out** of bed early.
8. He **knew** his neighbour's name.
9. He **wrote** a letter to his friend.
10. Max **thought** about his homework.

How Was Your Evening? (Page 110)
1. What
2. watched
3. it
4. so
5. was
6. about
7. was
8. Pretty
9. visited
10. listened

Unit 9

Tom's Vacation (Page 122)
A.
1. was
2. went
3. enjoyed
4. were
5. tried
6. ate
7. met
8. drove
9. took
10. bought
11. sent

B.
1. He went to Venezuela.
2. No, he went with a friend.
3. Yes, they did.
4. They were there for two weeks.
5. Yes, it was.
6. They stayed at a hotel.
7. They drove to some beautiful beaches.
8. Yes, they did.
9. They bought souvenirs.
10. He sent postcards to his friends.

On the Road (Page 122)
1. didn't fly
2. didn't take
3. didn't go
4. didn't stand
5. didn't think
6. didn't lose
7. didn't speak
8. didn't get
9. didn't tell
10. didn't buy

Questions and Answers (Page 123)
1. What did Roberto eat?
2. What did Carla buy?
3. What did Anne say?
4. What did Ali drink?
5. What did Max lose?

Prepositions (Page 123)
1. **in** 1993
2. **in** July
3. **in** winter
4. **on** weekends
5. **on** Monday
6. **on** March 5
7. **in** summer
8. **at** two o'clock
9. **at** 7:15
10. **on** May 1

Find the Errors (Page 123)
1. enjoied (enjoyed)
2. standed (stood)
3. buyed (bought)
4. drinked (drank)
5. brang (brought)

Unit 11

Count/Non-count Nouns (Page 142)
A.

Count singular	Count plural	Non-count
a chicken	some spoons	some money
a banana	some potatoes	some news
a cup	some plates	some soup
a stove	some forks	some sugar
an egg		some bread
a glass		some rice
an orange		some butter
a tomato		some salt

B.
1. some plates
2. an apple
3. some chairs
4. a knife
5. a glass
6. an orange
7. some eggs
8. a table
9. a fridge
10. some bread
11. an oven
12. some tomatoes
13. some onions
14. some sandwiches
15. a cup
16. a spoon
17. some bowls
18. an egg
19. some apples
20. a fork

In the Kitchen (Page 143)
A.
1. Is
2. are
3. Is
4. Are
5. are
6. Is
7. is
8. is
9. are
10. Is

B.
1. Please eat slowly.
2. Please add salt to the food.
3. Please put some butter on the table.
4. Please have some dessert.
5. Please don't be late.

C.
1. Let's go to the store.
2. Let's have dinner.
3. Let's drink coffee.
4. Let's use cups.
5. Let's open the window.

Spelling (Page 144)

1.	chicken	11.	spoon
2.	fridge	12.	kitchen
3.	water	13.	lettuce
4.	potatoes	14.	banana
5.	breakfast	15.	orange
6.	onion	16.	coffee
7.	sandwich	17.	bowl
8.	cheese	18.	refrigerator
9.	glasses	19.	apples
10.	knife	20.	oven

Unit 12

In the Park (Page 159)

A. 1. Max is sleeping under a tree.
   2. Nadia is writing a letter.
   3. Lili is listening to music.
   4. Joseph is reading a newspaper.
   5. Anne and Yumi are swimming in the lake.
   6. Roberto and Tom are playing soccer.

B. 1. The tourists aren't drinking coffee in the cafe.
   2. The taxi isn't stopping outside the hotel.
   3. They aren't listening to music.
   4. We aren't waiting at the bus stop.
   5. It isn't raining very hard today.
   6. The people aren't watching a movie on TV.
   7. I'm not looking for a telephone.
   8. He isn't walking to the bus stop.
   9. She isn't carrying a suitcase.
   10. They aren't taking pictures of their friends.

C. 1. Are   6. Is
   2. Is   7. Is
   3. Are   8. Is
   4. Am   9. Are
   5. Are   10. Are

Find the Owner (Page 160)

A. 1. This camera is his.
   2. These sunglasses are hers.
   3. This car is his.
   4. These keys are mine.
   5. These apples are ours.
   6. This umbrella is his.
   7. This apartment is his.
   8. These postcards are his.
   9. This wallet is hers.
   10. This chair is hers.

B. 1. They're hers.   6. They're yours.
   2. It's his.   7. It's his.
   3. It's his.   8. They're hers.
   4. They're his.   9. It's hers.
   5. It's hers.   10. It's his.

Unit 13

Then and Now (Page 174)

1. was living   6. were visiting
2. were speaking   7. was feeling
3. were watching   8. was doing
4. were travelling   9. was taking
5. was snowing   10. were living

Anne's Story (Page 175)

1. in 1990
2. at McGill University
3. medicine
4. very hard
5. in a drug store
6. She needed money to pay for her studies.

Vocabulary (Page 175)

1. slow   5. early
2. loud   6. first
3. bad   7. hard
4. tall   8. fat

Adverbs (Page 175)

1. quickly   6. quietly
2. hard   7. happily
3. loudly   8. hungrily
4. late   9. carefully
5. fast   10. quickly

Object Pronouns (Page 176)

1. him   6. them
2. her   7. her
3. them   8. him
4. us   9. him
5. her   10. them

Unit 14

Away from Home (Page 191)

1. I won't spend a lot of money.
2. I will write home often.
3. I won't be sad.
4. I won't forget my old friends.
5. I will make new friends.
6. I will be happy.
7. I will send postcards.
8. I will wear warm clothes.
9. I will eat good food.
10. I won't stay out late.

Making Plans (Page 191)

1. is going to relax
2. is going to take
3. is going to go
4. are going to eat
5. are going to buy

6. is going to take
7. is going to call
8. am going to change
9. are going to stop
10. is going to buy

Find the Errors (Page 192)

1. When **are** we **going to go** back to the hotel?
2. Who **is going to** study this evening?
3. They **are not going to** buy any fish today.
4. **Is it going to** rain tomorrow?
5. I **am going to walk** on the beach after dinner.

6. What **are you going to ask** the tour guide?
7. What time **is** the plane **going to** arrive?
8. Max **is not going to** travel next year.
9. Where **are we going to meet** this evening?
10. We **are not going to see** the new movie tonight.

Prepositions of Direction and Position (Page 192)

1. a
2. b
3. a
4. b
5. b
6. a

Answer Key

Unit 1

B. (Page 3)

1.	yes	6.	yes
2.	no	7.	no
3.	no	8.	no
4.	no	9.	yes
5.	yes	10.	yes

Understand: Greetings

A. (Page 4)

Possible answers:
1. Hello Dr. Martin. Hello Ms. Martin. Hello/Hi Anne.
2. Hello Mr. Kuslov. Hello/Hi Max.
3. Hello Ms. Suzuki. Hello/Hi Yumi.
4. Hello Mr. and Mrs. Lopez. Hello/Hi Carla and Roberto.
5. Hello Mr. Kirk. Hello/Hi Tom.
6. Hello Mr. and Mrs. Han. Hello/Hi Chen and Lili.
7. Hello Mr. and Mrs. Aziz. Hello/Hi Ali and Nadia.
8. Hello Mr. Muna. Hello/Hi Joseph.

Understand: Subject Pronouns

A. (Page 5)

The people are at the airport. They are passengers. A man is near the counter. He is Mr. Aziz from Cairo. A woman is near the suitcases. She is Carla Lopez from Mexico City. Two people are near the door. They are Mr. and Mrs. Han from Hong Kong.

B. (Page 5)

1.	she	6.	he
2.	they	7.	they
3.	they	8.	he
4.	she	9.	he
5.	he	10.	she

C. (Page 6)

1.	She	6.	Correct
2.	She	7.	It
3.	Correct	8.	They
4.	They	9.	Correct
5.	Correct	10.	They

Understand: Verb "Be"

A. (Page 7)

1.	is	6.	is
2.	is	7.	are
3.	are	8.	is
4.	is	9.	are
5.	am	10.	is

B. (Page 7)

1.	is	6.	are
2.	are	7.	is
3.	are	8.	are
4.	am	9.	are
5.	is	10.	are

C. (Page 7)

1.	are	6.	Correct
2.	is	7.	Correct
3.	Correct	8.	is
4.	am	9.	Correct
5.	are	10.	are

Understand: Plural Nouns

A. (Page 8)
1. teachers
2. tourists
3. children
4. people
5. suitcases
6. rooms
7. names
8. cameras
9. women
10. jobs
11. doctors
12. students
13. men
14. airports
15. girls
16. mothers

B. (Page 8)
1. women
2. children
3. hotels
4. Correct
5. tourists
6. child
7. suitcases
8. Correct
9. people
10. Correct

Understand: Verb "Be" Contraction

A. (Page 9)
1. a
2. i
3. a
4. i
5. a
6. a
7. i

B. (Page 9)
1. She's
2. I'm
3. He's
4. You're
5. We're
6. He's
7. They're
8. You're

Nice to Meet You (Page 10)

Conversation 1
Nadia: Hello. My name is Nadia. I'm from Egypt.
Anne: **Hi** Nadia. Nice to meet you. **I'm** Anne. I'm from Canada.
Nadia: **I'm** pleased to meet you, Anne.
Anne: I'm pleased **to** meet you too, Nadia.

Conversation 2
Tom: Hello. I'm Tom. I'm **from** the United States.
Yumi: Hi Tom. **Nice** to meet you. My name is Yumi.
Tom: Are you from Japan, Yumi?
Yumi: Yes, **I'm** from Kyoto, Japan.
Tom: I'm pleased to **meet** you.

How's It Going? (Page 10)

Max: Hi. How's **it** going, Ali?
Ali: Okay. How **about** you, Max?
Max: Pretty good. **How's** your new job?
Ali: **Not** bad. It's a good job.

Unit 2

Words You Need (Page 16)
1. No
2. Yes
3. Yes
4. Yes
5. No
6. No
7. Yes
8. Yes

Understand: "Be" Question Form

A. (Page 17)
1. Are they Taiwanese?
2. Is Mr. Lopez Spanish?
3. Is she a teacher?
4. Are you tourists?
5. Is Yumi Japanese?
6. Is Tom American?
7. Is she a doctor?
8. Am I late?
9. Is Nadia Aziz an engineer?
10. Are they happy?

B. (Page 18)
Possible questions:
1. Is Yumi Suzuki Japanese?
2. Is Yumi Suzuki 24 years old?
3. Is Yumi Suzuki a teacher?
4. Is Chen Han Chinese?
5. Is Chen Han 31 years old?
6. Is Chen Han a photographer?
7. Is Nadia Aziz Egyptian?
8. Is Nadia Aziz 25 years old?
9. Is Nadia Aziz an engineer?

Understand: "Be" Negative (Page 18)

A. (Page 18)
1. I am not Canadian.
2. He is not American.
3. They are not Japanese.
4. She is not French.
5. We are not Korean.
6. She is not Australian.
7. He is not Italian.
8. They are not Turkish.
9. She is not Chinese.
10. They are not Brazilian.

B. (Page 19)
1. not
2. I
3. is
4. not
5. are
6. not
7. am
8. not
9. are
10. is

Understand: "Be" Contraction

A. (Page 19)
1. I'm not
2. he's not
3. you're not
4. it's not
5. they're not
6. she's not

B. (Page 20)
1. She isn't Chinese.
2. It isn't small.
3. They aren't French.
4. I'm not in England.
5. We aren't tourists.
6. He isn't a bus driver.
7. He isn't an engineer.
8. He isn't six years old.
9. You aren't Canadian.
10. It isn't big.

Understand: "Be" Short Answers (Page 21)

1. Yes, she is.
2. No, he isn't.
3. No, they aren't.
4. Yes, you are.
5. Yes, you are.
6. Yes, they are.
7. No, we aren't.
8. No, she isn't.
9. Yes, he is.
10. Yes, I am.

Special Uses of "It is"

A. (Page 22)
1. New York: It is twelve o'clock. (It is noon. It is midnight).
2. Vancouver: It is nine o'clock.
3. Tokyo: It is two o'clock.
4. Paris: It is six o'clock.
5. London: It is five o'clock.

B. (Page 22)
1. It's 3:10.
2. It's Monday.
3. It's April 15.
4. It's September.
5. It's spring.
6. It's 19_____.

C. (Page 22)
1. No, it isn't.
2. No, it isn't.
3. Yes, it is.
4. No, it isn't.
5. Yes, it is.
6. Yes, it is.
7. No, it isn't.
8. Yes, it is.
9. No, it isn't.
10. Yes, it is.

I've Got to Go Now

B. (Page 23)
1. No, it isn't.
2. Yes, he is.

C. (Page 24)
Chen: What time is **it**?
Lili: It's 8 o'clock.
Chen: Oh. I've **got** to go now. I'm late for work.
Lili: Have a **nice** day.
Chen: You too.

It's Freezing Today

B. (Page 24)
Carla: Hi. How**'s** it going?
Tom: Not bad.
Carla: **Pretty** cold weather, eh?
Tom: It sure is. **It's** freezing today.
Carla: Yeah, winter is really cold in Canada.
Tom: Well, see **you** later.
Carla: 'Bye.

C. (Page 25)
Carla: Hi. **How's** it going?
Tom: **Not** bad.
Carla: Pretty cold weather, eh?
Tom: It sure is. **It's** freezing today.
Carla: **Yeah**, winter is really cold in Canada.
Tom: Well, see you later.
Carla: 'Bye.

Unit 3

Words You Need (Page 31)

1. A, B, C
2. B
3. B, C
4. B, C
5. C
6. B, C
7. A
8. A, B, C
9. A
10. C
11. A
12. A
13. C
14. A, B

Understand: Demonstrative Adjectives

A. (Page 32)
1. This
2. Those
3. Those
4. This
5. That
6. Those
7. These
8. This
9. That
10. That

B. (Page 32)
1. These
2. Correct
3. Correct
4. This
5. Correct
6. Correct
7. This
8. Correct
9. Correct
10. Correct

C. (Page 33)
1. c
2. h
3. a
4. f
5. e
6. i
7. d
8. g
9. b
10. j

Understand: "Be" Simple Past Tense

A. (Page 34)

1. was
2. were
3. Correct
4. were
5. was
6. was
7. was
8. were
9. were
10. Correct

B. (Page 34)

1. at work
2. at home
3. at school

C. (Page 34)

1. at the hospital
2. at the post office
3. at the drugstore
4. at the movies
5. at the restaurant
6. at the supermarket
7. at the dentist
8. at the bank

Understand: "Be" Simple Past Negative

A. (Page 36)

1. He wasn't tired.
2. They weren't late.
3. It wasn't cold yesterday.
4. I wasn't wrong.
5. She wasn't tall.
6. They weren't Japanese.
7. We weren't lost.
8. It wasn't at two o'clock.
9. You weren't happy.
10. She wasn't American.

B. (Page 36)

Yesterday I was not happy. Everything **was** wrong. The hotel was busy. People **were** not on time. The tour bus **was** late. It was not big. We **were** not comfortable. The tour guide was not polite. The weather **was** bad. People **were** not happy.

Understand: Expressions of Past Time (Page 37)

1. last Wednesday
2. last Friday
3. yesterday
4. last Thursday
5. last Sunday
6. on Sunday
7. last Monday
8. Saturday

What a Nice Family!

B. (Page 38)

1. Yes, he is.
2. No, he isn't.
3. Yes, she is.

C. (Page 38)

Anne: Is this a picture **of** your family, Lili?
Lili: Yes, it is. That's my husband on the left.
Anne: Are those your **children**?
Lili: Yes, they are.

Anne: How **old** are they?
Lili: My son is five and my daughter is three.
Anne: What **a** nice family!

Hurry Up, We're Late!

B. (Page 39)

Nadia: Hurry **up**, Ali. We're late.
Ali: Where is my camera?
Nadia: It's **over** there.
Ali: Where are my keys?
Nadia: They're **right** here.
Ali: Okay. Let**'s** go.

Unit 4

Words You Need (Page 44)

1. b
2. l
3. f
4. c
5. g
6. a
7. h
8. j
9. k
10. i
11. d
12. e

Understand: "Can" to Express Ability

A. (Page 45)

1. Yumi can play the piano.
2. Carla can cook rice.
3. Joseph can drive a car.
4. Lili can use a camera.
5. Tom and Max can play tennis.
6. Chen can play the piano.
7. Anne can use a washing machine.
8. Nadia can speak Arabic and Spanish.
9. Max can drive to school.
10. Chen and Lili can eat with chopsticks.

B. (Page 45)

1. from a cup
2. with a camera
3. with a pencil
4. in a car
5. with a guitar
6. from a book
7. with chopsticks
8. on a telephone

Understand: "Can" Negative

A. (Page 46)

1. I cannot speak Japanese.
2. He cannot drive a bus.
3. She cannot write.
4. They cannot read French.
5. We cannot cook spaghetti.
6. You cannot play piano.
7. I cannot carry that suitcase.
8. We cannot eat with a fork.
9. He cannot use a washing machine.
10. She cannot use a computer.

B. (Page 46)
1. Lili can't use a camera.
2. Max can't drive a truck.
3. They can't read Spanish.
4. She can't play soccer.
5. It can't walk.
6. Joseph can't cook eggs.
7. Roberto can't speak two languages.
8. Yumi can't play tennis.
9. You can't read Hungarian.
10. They can't understand me.

Understand : "Can" Question Form

A. (Page 47)

1.	e	4.	c
2.	f	5.	b
3.	a	6.	d

B. (Page 48)
1. Can you play tennis?
2. Can you speak two languages?
3. Can you cook rice?
4. Can you use a computer?
5. Can you drive a car?
6. Can you play soccer?
7. Can you use a camera?
8. Can you speak Japanese?
9. Can you eat with chopsticks?
10. Can you drive a truck?

Understand: Indefinite Articles

A. (Page 49)

1. a teacher		6. an orderly
2. an engineer		7. a clerk
3. a mechanic		8. a cashier
4. a librarian		9. an artist
5. a teller		10. a doctor

B. (Page 49)

1. a teacher		6. an orderly
2. an engineer		7. a clerk
3. a mechanic		8. a cashier
4. a librarian		9. an artist
5. a teller		10. a doctor

Understand: Possessive Adjectives

A. (Page 50)

1. our		6. their
2. his		7. her
3. my		8. their/your
4. her		9. his
5. their		10. your

B. (Page 51)

1. their		4. her
2. his		5. his
3. his		

C. (Page 51)

1. our		4. her
2. my		5. your
3. his		

Can I Leave My Number?

B. (Page 52)

1. b		3. c
2. a		

C. (Page 52)

Yumi: Hello. Can I speak **to** Max please?
Father: **Sorry**, he isn't home.
Yumi: This is Yumi. Can I leave my number?
Father: Sure. What **is** the number?
Yumi: It's 731-2878.
Father: Can you repeat **that**?
Yumi: Sure. It's 731-2878.

Sorry, Wrong Number

B. (Page 53)

Carla: Hello. Anne?
Woman: Anne?
Carla: Yes, can I speak to Anne please?
Woman: **I'm** sorry. You have the wrong number.
Carla: Is **this** 326-1769?
Woman: No, it isn't.
Carla: Excuse me.
Woman: That's okay. **It's** no problem.

Unit 5

A. (Page 58)

Family Name:	Muna
First Name:	Joseph
Age:	25
Sex:	male
Country:	Cameroon
Languages:	English, French, Ewondo
Occupation:	accountant

Family Name:	Lopez
First Name:	Roberto
Age:	29
Sex:	male
Country:	Mexico
Languages:	Spanish, English
Occupation:	orderly

Family Name: Kuslov
First Name: Max
Age: 19
Sex: male
Country: Russia
Languages: Russian, English
Occupation: mechanic

Family Name: Han
First Name: Lili
Age: 25
Sex: female
Country: Hong Kong
Languages: Cantonese, English
Occupation: bank teller

Family Name: Suzuki
First Name: Yumi
Age: 24
Sex: female
Country: Japan
Languages: Japanese, English
Occupation: teacher

Family Name: Aziz
First Name: Nadia
Age: 34
Sex: female
Country: Egypt
Languages: Arabic, English
Occupation: engineer

Family Name: Kirk
First Name: Tom
Age: 28
Sex: male
Country: United States
Languages: English, Japanese
Occupation: flight attendant

B. (Page 59)
1. French, English
2. 27
3. He is an accountant.
4. Russian, English
5. No, he isn't.
6. 25
7. Kyoto
8. Egyptian
9. 34
10. Los Angeles, United States

Country and Nationality

A. (Page 59)
1. French
2. Chinese
3. Spanish
4. Canadian
5. Vietnamese
6. American
7. Turkish
8. Indonesian
9. Brazilian
10. Australian

Check In (Page 60)
1. Can
2. are
3. My
4. My
5. Where

New Friends (Page 60)
1. My
2. Nice
3. is
4. meet
5. Where
6. It

Families

A. (Page 60)
1. brother
2. uncle
3. grandfather
4. husband
5. father
6. grandson
7. son

B. (Page 61)
Last Saturday afternoon was fun. The weather **was** hot and sunny. My family and I **were** in a new city. We **were** tourists. My father **was** the driver. My sister **was** the tour guide. My brother **was** the photographer. The afternoon **was** fun. We **were** happy.

Postcards from Banff (Page 61)
1. yes (Yes, they can.)
2. 26
3. play tennis, swim
4. It is beautiful.
5. listen to music
6. on the weekend
7. last winter
8. in a big, old hotel
9. Joe
10. three languages

Unit 6

Words You Need (Page 64)
1. A
2. C
3. C
4. A, B
5. B, C
6. A
7. B
8. A
9. A, B, C
10. C

Understand: Verb "Have"

A. (Page 66)
1. Correct
2. Correct
3. Correct
4. have
5. Correct
6. has
7. have
8. Correct
9. have
10. has

B. (Page 66)
1. have
2. have
3. has
4. have
5. has
6. has
7. has
8. have
9. have
10. have

C. (Page 66)
1. Susan
2. Pierre
3. Jill
4. Ellen
5. Carlos
6. Ray, Julia
7. Rita
8. Maria, Don
9. Ralph
10. Bob, Karen

Understand: "Have" Negative Contraction

A. (Page 68)
1. Max doesn't have a moustache.
2. He doesn't have a wife.
3. Carla doesn't have long hair.
4. Lili and Chen don't have a daughter.
5. Nadia doesn't have blue eyes.
6. Anne doesn't have a dog.
7. Yumi doesn't have a big family.
8. They don't have a big apartment.
9. We don't have short hair.
10. Tom doesn't have an old car.

B. (Page 68)
1. have
2. Correct
3. doesn't
4. don't
5. Correct
6. Correct
7. don't
8. have
9. Correct
10. doesn't

Understand: Using "Any" in Negative Sentences

A. (Page 69)
1. We don't have any friends in Italy.
2. Max doesn't have any pictures of his family.
3. Lili doesn't have any cousins in China.
4. That school doesn't have any English classes.
5. Montreal doesn't have any hot days in winter.
6. Yumi doesn't have any apples.
7. I don't have any relatives in Los Angeles.
8. Our new apartment doesn't have any big windows.
9. Anne doesn't have any sisters.
10. Our class doesn't have any students from Korea.

B. (Page 69)
1. some
2. any
3. some
4. some
5. any
6. any
7. any
8. some
9. some
10. any

Understand: "Have" Question Form

A. (Page 70)
1. Does he have a new bicycle?
2. Do we have a good teacher?
3. Does she have a friend in Texas?
4. Do they have a new house?
5. Does Roberto have a new car?
6. Does his brother have a moustache?
7. Do they have a child?
8. Does Anne have short hair?
9. Do Nadia and Lili have long hair?
10. Does Kyoto have a good climate?

B. (Page 70)
1. Yes, he does.
2. Yes, it does.
3. Yes, he does.
4. No, he doesn't.
5. Yes, it does.
6. Yes, they do.
7. No, they don't.

Understand: Spelling Plural Nouns Ending in "y"

A. (Page 71)
1. friends
2. cities
3. brothers
4. children
5. students
6. women
7. countries
8. days
9. cousins
10. parties
11. families
12. keys

B. (Page 72)

Understand: Possessive Nouns

A. (Page 73)
1. Anne's office
2. Chen's apartment
3. Joseph's living room
4. Roberto's house
5. Lili's brother
6. the teacher's glasses
7. Nadia's sister
8. Tom's camera
9. Carla's daughter
10. Yumi's fridge

B (Page 74)
a. Yumi's suitcase
b. Tom's bicycle
c. Anne's sunglasses
d. Lili's hat
e. Yumi's purse
f. Roberto's soccer ball
g. Chen's telephone
h. Joseph's guitar
i. Anne's keys
j. Anne's books
k. Carla's camera
l. Max's tennis racket

Do You Have an Apartment for Rent?

B. (Page 75)
1. a
2. b
3. a
4. b

C. (Page 75)
Lili: Hello. Do you have **an** apartment for rent?
Landlord: Yes, I do. It has four rooms.
Lili: **Does** it have two bedrooms?
Landlord: No, it doesn't. It **has** one bedroom.
Lili: Oh, It's **too** small. I have two kids. Thanks anyway.

I've Got a New Place

B. (Page 76)
1. a
2. b

C. (Page 76)
Yumi: I've got a new **place**.
Anne: That's great. What's it like?
Yumi: It's **got** a nice kitchen, but I don't have a kitchen table.
Anne: Oh, I've got a small table. You **can** have it.
Yumi: Thanks a **lot**!

Unit 7

Words You Need

A. (Page 82)
1. f
2. c
3. g
4. d
5. e
6. b
7. a
8. h

B. (Page 82)
1. 7:00
2. 8:00
3. 7:45
4. 7:15
5. 8:25
6. 8:20
7. 7:30
8. 9:00

Understand: Simple Present Tense

A. (Page 83)
1. drink
2. wakes up
3. works
4. walks
5. drive
6. eats
7. watch
8. takes
9. goes
10. go

B. (Page 84)
1. e
2. g
3. a
4. h
5. f
6. i
7. d
8. b
9. c
10. j

C. (Page 85)
1. gets up
2. eats
3. leaves
4. drives
5. walks
6. finishes
7. watches

Understand: Simple Present Tense Negative

A. (Page 86)
1. Correct
2. doesn't eat
3. don't walk
4. doesn't go
5. Correct
6. don't speak
7. Correct
8. don't talk
9. doesn't go
10. don't work

B. (Page 86)
1. Tourists don't get up early.
2. Nadia and Ali don't take pictures.
3. They don't eat dinner at home.
4. He doesn't write letters to his parents.
5. We don't stay home in the evening.
6. She doesn't buy postcards in the hotel.
7. Max doesn't walk in the city.
8. Tourists don't go to bed early.
9. People don't go to the beach at night.
10. Anne doesn't drive the tour bus.

Understand: Present Simple Question Form

A. (Page 87)
1. Does Tom know the people in the hotel?
2. Does she work in the hotel?
3. Do the tourists meet in the lobby?
4. Do Anne and Yumi go shopping?
5. Does Carla take pictures of the group?
6. Does the tour begin at two o'clock?
7. Do we need our keys after 11 o'clock?
8. Does the restaurant serve good food?
9. Does Yumi write to her family?
10. Does Joseph eat breakfast early?

B. (Page 87)

1. Correct
2. Does
3. Correct
4. know
5. Do
6. Correct
7. Correct
8. work
9. Does
10. come

C. (Page 87)

1. does
2. I
3. do
4. doesn't
5. they
6. she does
7. they do
8. don't
9. doesn't
10. it

Understand: Adverbs of Frequency

A. (Page 88)

1. sometimes meet
2. Correct
3. sometimes takes
4. are never
5. is sometimes
6. Correct
7. usually speaks
8. often takes
9. Correct
10. Correct

B. (Page 88)

1. People on vacation usually get up late.
2. The weather in Thailand is never cold.
3. The restaurant sometimes serves seafood.
4. Tourists usually take photographs.
5. The weather is always hot and humid in Panama.
6. The temperature in Montreal often changes quickly.
7. People in that hotel are usually tourists.
8. We never eat before seven.
9. They always take pictures of the sunset.
10. He sometimes eats in that restaurant.

Understand: Prepositions of Place

A. (Page 89)

1. on
2. beside
3. between
4. in
5. on
6. under
7. beside
8. under
9. in
10. beside

B. (Page 90)

1. The pen in under the box.
2. The apple is in the box
3. The telephone is beside the box.
4. The keys are on the box.
5. The TV is beside the box.
6. The pictures are in the box.
7. The guitar is in the box.
8. The books are on the box.
9. The umbrella is under the box.
10. The camera is between the box and the book.

Does This Bus Go Downtown?

B. (Page 91)

1. No, it doesn't.
2. Yes, it does.

C. (Page 91)

Max: Excuse **me**. Does the 129 bus go downtown?
Bus driver: No it doesn't.
Max: Oh. What bus **goes** downtown?
Bus driver: The 51 bus. You **get** it over there.
Max: Thanks a lot.
Bus driver: **No** problem.

Do You Want a Lift?

B. (Page 91)

1. c
2. b
3. c

C. (Page 92)

Max: **How** do you come to work every day?
Joseph: I usually take the bus. **What** about you?
Max: I drive to work.
Joseph: Where do you live?
Max: I live downtown.
Joseph: Me **too**.
Max: Do you want a **lift** sometimes?
Joseph: Sure. Thanks a lot.

Unit 8

Words You Need (Page 98)

1. b
2. e
3. a
4. h
5. i
6. j
7. d
8. c
9. f
10. g

Understand: Simple Past Tense

A. (Page 99)

1. walked
2. played
3. answered
4. talked
5. watched
6. arrived
7. listened
8. started
9. telephoned
10. turned off

B. (Page 100)

1. arrived
2. turned on
3. shouted
4. cooked
5. served
6. opened
7. thanked
8. played
9. listened
10. ended

Understand: Pronouncing Past Tense Verb Endings

B. (Page 101)

1. worked	7. played
2. washed	8. closed
3. asked	9. wanted
4. watched	10. needed
5. arrived	11. started
6. closed	12. tasted

Understand: Spelling Past Tense Verbs

A. (Page 103)

1. watched TV	9. waited for a taxi
2. turned on the light	10. called your friend
3. enjoyed the movie	11. stayed at home
4. listened to music	12. lived in Argentina
5. stopped the cassette	13. missed the bus
6. tried some rice	14. carried a suitcase
7. closed the window	15. washed your car
8. planned a party	16. studied for an exam

B. (Page 103)

1. stopped	6. carried
2. Correct	7. Correct
3. Correct	8. Correct
4. planned	9. studied
5. Correct	10. Correct

C. (Page 103)

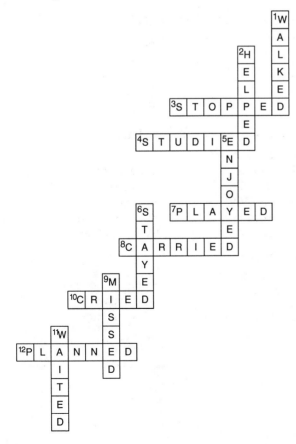

Understand: Simple Past Tense Negative

A. (Page 104)

1. The tourists didn't visit the city.
2. I didn't talk to my friend at breakfast.
3. She didn't like the food in that restaurant.
4. It didn't rain yesterday.
5. The party didn't end at 11 o'clock.
6. They didn't play soccer this morning.
7. Nadia and Ali didn't watch TV last night.
8. We didn't arrive at the bus stop on time.
9. Tom didn't carry our suitcases.
10. We didn't talk to the pilot.

B. (Page 105)

1. He didn't finish his homework.
2. He didn't listen to his new cassette.
3. He didn't watch the news on TV.
4. He didn't finish a letter home.
5. He didn't practise piano.
6. He didn't go to a movie.
7. He didn't visit friends.

Understand: Simple Past Question Form

A. (Page 106)

1. Did they look nice?
2. Did you answer the phone?
3. Did she ask the question?
4. Did the bus stop here?
5. Did they wash the dishes?
6. Did I learn Spanish in Mexico?
7. Did Anne want help?
8. Did he phone home last night?
9. Did the bus turn right?
10. Did they need a map?

B. (Page 106)

1. phone	6. Correct
2. answer	7. telephone
3. Correct	8. Correct
4. want	9. want
5. watch	10. Correct

What Did You Do Yesterday?

B. (Page 107)

1. Max
2. stayed home all day
3. visited a friend, watched TV

C. (Page 107)

Tom: Hello. Is Max **there** please?

Max: Speaking.

Tom: Hi Max. **This** is Tom. What did you do yesterday?

Max: Yesterday? Oh, nothing **special**. I stayed home all day. What **about** you?

Tom: I visited a friend. Then I watched TV at night.

How Was Your Weekend?

B. (Page 108)

worked, cleaned the house, washed the car

C. (Page 108)

Anne: Hi Roberto. How was your weekend?
Roberto: So **so**. I worked on Saturday.
Anne: Did you finish your work?
Roberto: Yes, **I** did. Then I cleaned the house and washed the car.
Anne: **Boy**! You had a busy weekend.
Roberto: I sure did. Now I need a **rest**!

Unit 9

Words You Need (Page 112)

1. Lili
2. Anne
3. Max
4. Yumi
5. Tom
6. Nadia
7. Carla
8. Chen
9. Joseph
10. Roberto

Understand: Simple Past Tense Irregular Form

A. (Page 113)

1. I wrote to my mother.
2. They drank coffee after dinner.
3. He met his friend after class.
4. You sat near me in class.
5. We ate in that restaurant.
6. She slept in the bus.
7. He brought his homework to class.
8. They bought postcards for their friends.
9. People stood in line at the bank.
10. I got letters from home.

B. (Page 113)

1. did
2. sat
3. wrote
4. drank
5. bought
6. slept
7. brought
8. stood
9. ate
10. took
11. met

Understand: Simple Past Tense Irregular Negative

A. (Page 114)

1. He didn't go to Bali on vacation.
2. They didn't send us three postcards.
3. Her friend didn't speak Spanish.
4. We didn't tell them our names.
5. I didn't think it was an old camera.
6. The plane didn't leave at eight o'clock.
7. They didn't come from China.
8. Tom didn't drive here from Los Angeles.
9. The tour didn't begin at two o'clock.
10. Anne didn't fly here from Paris.

B. (Page 115)

Lili: We met some interesting people yesterday. They spoke Spanish.
Chen: They didn't **speak** Spanish, Lili. They **spoke** Italian.
Lili: Well, they flew here from Madrid.
Chen: They didn't **fly** here from Madrid. They **flew** here from Rome.
Lili: They thought we were Japanese tourists.
Chen: They didn't **think** we were Japanese tourists. They **thought** we were Korean.
Lili: Well anyway, I told them that we came here last weekend.
Chen: We didn't **come** here last weekend. We **came** here on Thursday.
Lili: Okay, Chen. You **tell** the story.

Understand: Simple Past Tense Irregular Question Form

A. (Page 116)

1. Did I find some sunglasses in the lobby?
2. Did they see their friend in the street?
3. Did he put the suitcase in the bus?
4. Did the clerk sell me some flowers?
5. Did Yumi give her a present?
6. Did we wear our raincoats?
7. Did Robert lose his wallet in the store?
8. Did the guide know our names?
9. Did the bus driver make a left turn?
10. Did the bus ticket cost one dollar?

B. (Page 116)

1. say
2. didn't leave
3. Correct
4. tell
5. Correct
6. Correct
7. Correct
8. didn't know
9. Correct
10. Correct

Understand: Prepositions of Time

A. (Page 117)

1. Anne met Yumi on June 12.
2. Anne got up early on Wednesday.
3. Anne saw the travel agent on June 5.
4. Anne made reservations for the hotel on June 8.
5. Anne left on her trip on Saturday.
6. Anne took the train to Vancouver on June 17.
7. Anne flew home on Friday.
8. Anne sent postcards on June 18.
9. Anne bought stamps on Monday.
10. Anne's vacation finished on June 30.

B. (Page 118)

1. on	6. on
2. at	7. on
3. on	8. at
4. in	9. in
5. on	10. in

Understand: Plural Nouns with "es"

A. (Page 118)

1. cameras	9. telephones
2. watches	10. days
3. men	11. families
4. children	12. glasses
5. dishes	13. cities
6. people	14. boxes
7. parties	15. friends
8. women	16. countries

B. (Page 118)

1. watches	6. Correct
2. Correct	7. women
3. Correct	8. countries
4. families	9. Correct
5. sunglasses	10. dishes

Late for Work

B. (Page 119)

1. b	3. c
2. b	4. b

C. (Page 119)

Max: Hi Roberto. **How** was your day?
Roberto: Terrible. I was late for work this morning.
Max: How **come**?
Roberto: I missed my bus. Then I waited 20 minutes for the next bus.
Max: **Was** your boss angry?
Roberto: Yeah, he was really **mad**.

A Terrible Day

B. (Page 120)

1. b	3. a
2. b	4. b

C. (Page 120)

Joseph: Hi Tom. How **was** your day?
Tom: Terrible. My car didn't start this morning.
Joseph: That's **too** bad. What did you do?
Tom: I called the garage.
Joseph: How did you **get** to work?
Tom: I got a lift with Roberto.
Joseph: That's lucky.

Unit 10

Simple Past Tense

A. (Page 126)

1. She watched a movie Saturday afternoon.
2. She washed the car Sunday morning.
3. She cleaned the house Saturday morning.
4. She worked in the office Friday afternoon.
5. She listened to music Saturday night.

B. (Page 126)

1. She cleaned the house.
2. She talked on the phone.
3. She finished a letter.
4. She visited friends.
5. She listened to music.

Simple Past Tense Irregular Form

A. (Page 126)

1. at six o'clock yesterday
2. They took a bus.
3. near the swimming pool
4. No, they didn't.
5. after the trip
6. in the restaurant
7. Yes, they did.
8. They were from Canada.
9. coffee

B. (Page 127)

begin	began
bring	brought
buy	bought
come	came
cost	cost
do	did
drink	drank
drive	drove
eat	ate
find	found
fly	flew
get	got
give	gave
go	went
know	knew
lose	lost
make	made
meet	met
put	put
say	said
see	saw
sell	sold
send	sent
sit	sat
sleep	slept
speak	spoke
stand	stood

226

swim	swam
take	took
tell	told
think	thought
understand	understood
wear	wore
write	wrote

C. (Page 128)

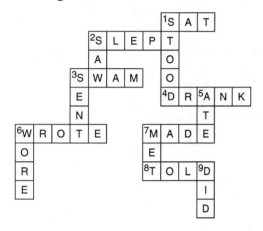

Spelling (Page 128)

1. swam
2. enjoyed
3. drank
4. families
5. ate
6. bought
7. keys
8. came
9. took
10. cities

Questions with "How" and "Where" (Page 128)

Relatives	How did they come?	Where did they come from?
parents	flew	Los Angeles
sister	drove	San Diego
cousin	train	Winnipeg
grandparents	bus	Portland
brother	ferry, bus	Victoria

Unit 11

Words You Need (Page 130)

1. g
2. u
3. f
4. b
5. a
6. i
7. p
8. m
9. q
10. h
11. j
12. k
13. l
14. t
15. r
16. n
17. s
18. o
19. c
20. e
21. d

Understand: Count and Non-count Nouns

A. (Page 131)

1. an apple
2. some eggs
3. a bowl
4. a knife
5. a carrot
6. some onions
7. a refrigerator
8. some spoons
9. an orange
10 a plate
11. some glasses
12. some apples
13. a kitchen
14. an oven
15. some sandwiches
16. some oranges
17. an egg
18. some plates
19. an onion
20. a glass

B. (Page 132)

Count	Non-count
eggs	meat
glasses	spaghetti
orange	cereal
tomato	rice
spoons	water
oven	salt
knife	fruit
banana	lettuce
plates	sugar
onions	
cups	

C. (Page 133)

1. an egg
2. a tomato
3. some bread
4. some coffee
5. some sugar
6. a table
7. an apple
8. some salt
9. a banana
10. some milk
11. some potatoes
12. some muffins
13. some forks
14. some water
15. a stove
16. some spoons
17. a refrigerator
18. some rice
19. some butter
20 a glass

Understand: "There" + "Be"

A. (Page 134)

1. There is
2. There are
3. There is
4. There is
5. There are
6. There is
7. There is
8. There is
9. There is
10. There are

B. (Page 134)

Possible answers:
1. There is some milk.
2. There is some cheese.
3. There are some eggs.
4. There is some yoghurt.
5. There is some butter.
6. There is some fish.
7. There is some meat.

8. There is some orange juice.
9. There are some vegetables.
10. There is some fruit.
11. There are some apples.
12. There is a lemon.
13. There are some oranges.
14. There are some carrots.
15. There is some lettuce.
16. There are some tomatoes.
17. There are some potatoes.
18. There is an onion.
19. There is some ketchup.
20. There is some mustard.

Understand: "There" + "Be" Negative

A. (Page 135)
1. There isn't any bread on the counter.
2. There aren't any apples on the table.
3. There isn't any butter in the sandwich.
4. There aren't any tomatoes in this sandwich.
5. There isn't any sugar in my tea.
6. There aren't any apples at the supermarket.
7. There aren't any sandwiches on the table.
8. There aren't any oranges in that bowl.
9. There isn't any milk in the refrigerator.
10. There isn't any coffee in this cup.

B. (Page 135)
1. There isn't	6. There aren't
2. There aren't	7. There aren't
3. There isn't	8. There isn't
4. There isn't	9. There aren't
5. There isn't	10. There aren't

Understand: "There" + "Be" Question Form

A. (Page 136)
1. Is there a chicken on the stove?
2. Are there any oranges in that bag?
3. Are there any potatoes with the chicken?
4. Is there a spoon on the counter?
5. Are there any forks in that drawer?
6. Is there any lettuce in that sandwich?
7. Is there a cup on the table?
8. Are there any apples in the refrigerator?
9. Are there any glasses in the cupboard?
10. Is there any milk in my coffee?

B. (Page 136)
1. Yes, there is.	6. Yes, there are.
2. Yes, there is.	7. Yes, there is.
3. No, there isn't.	8. Yes, there are.
4. Yes, there are.	9. No, there isn't.
5. No, there aren't.	10. No, there isn't.

Understand: Imperatives

A. (Page 138)
1. e	4. d
2. c	5. b
3. a	6. f

B. (Page 138)
1. e	4. f
2. a	5. b
3. d	6. c

Understand: "Let's" for Suggestions (Page 139)
1. g	6. h
2. i	7. e
3. f	8. b
4. a	9. d
5. j	10. c

What's for Supper?

B. (Page 140)
some chicken, some rice, some salad

C. (Page 140)
Ali: Nadia, I'm hungry. What's **for** supper?
Nadia: Well, there's some chicken in the fridge.
Ali: Is there **any** rice?
Nadia: Yes, there is. There's some in a bowl. I can heat it **up**.
Ali: Is there anything **else** in the fridge?
Nadia: Yes, there's some salad.

What a Great Party!

B. (Page 141)
Max: **What** a great party! The food looks delicious.
Tom: Let's **try** the chicken. It looks really good.
Max: What's for dessert?
Tom: There's a chocolate cake.
Max: **I'm** starving. Come **on**. Let's eat!

Unit 12

Words You Need (Page 146)
1. g	7. d
2. a	8. i
3. b	9. e
4. j	10. k
5. c	11. l
6. h	12. f

Present Continuous Aspect

A. (Page 148)
1. c	5. e
2. b	6. d
3. a	7. g
4. f	

B. (Page 149)

1. are shopping
2. Correct
3. is trying
4. is paying
5. Correct
6. am shopping
7. Correct
8. are leaving
9. is carrying
10. Correct

C. (Page 149)

1. are selling
2. is helping
3. is trying on
4. is waiting
5. is talking
6. are buying
7. are paying

D. (Page 149)

1. the department store
2. Nadia
3. Anne
4. at the department store
5. a dress
6. a new blouse
7. some T-shirts
8. with a credit card

Understand: Spelling Verbs Ending with "ing"

A. (Page 150)

1. We are eating dinner late.
2. I am waking up early.
3. He is studying hard.
4. They are getting off the bus.
5. You are sitting in the bus.
6. He is putting his wallet into his pocket.
7. I am smiling at my friends.
8. We are reading in the library.
9. She is waiting for the bus near home.
10. They are working for the bank.

B. (Page 151)

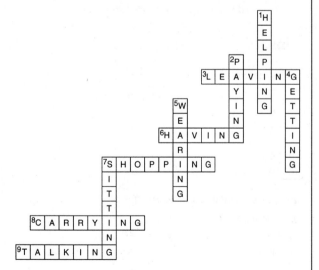

Understand: Present Continuous Negative

A. (Page 152)

1. Joseph isn't taking pictures this afternoon.
2. Anne isn't eating alone tonight.
3. Chen isn't talking to the bus driver now.
4. Max isn't watching TV this morning.
5. Nadia and Carla aren't playing tennis today.
6. Yumi isn't smiling at the camera at the moment.
7. Tom and Roberto aren't wearing jeans right now.
8. Lili isn't wearing a sweater this evening.
9. Anne and Yumi aren't having coffee in that cafe at the moment.
10. Ali and Nadia aren't listening to the news after dinner tonight.

B. (Page 152)

1. Chen and Lili aren't buying T-shirts. They are buying shoes.
2. Yumi isn't trying on a dress. She is trying on a jacket.
3. Roberto isn't looking at jackets. He is looking at coats.
4. Joseph isn't wearing a shirt. He is wearing a sweater.
5. Ali and Nadia aren't carrying coats. They are carrying T-shirts.
6. Carla isn't holding a blouse. She is holding a sweater.

Understand: Present Continuous Question Form

A. (Page 154)

1. Are you sleeping?
2. Are we looking for Tom?
3. Is Yumi writing to her sister?
4. Is he wearing new shoes?
5. Are they waiting for the bus?
6. Is Nadia trying on that jacket?
7. Are you visiting the city?
8. Is Anne carrying that big suitcase alone?
9. Are Tom and Roberto speaking Spanish?
10. Are you looking for her glasses?

B. (Page 154)

1. Is Max listening to music?
2. Correct
3. Is she watching a movie?
4. Are Nadia and Ali eating lunch now?
5. Are you buying postcards for your family?
6. Correct
7. Correct
8. Correct
9. Is Tom having dinner in a restaurant?
10. Correct

Understand: Possessive Pronouns

A. (Page 155)
1. his
2. ours
3. theirs
4. mine
5. yours
6. hers

B. (Page 155)
1. my
2. hers
3. our
4. your
5. my
6. his
7. their
8. mine
9. yours
10. their

C. (Page 156)
1. They're hers.
2. It's his.
3. It's hers.
4. It's his.
5. They're theirs.
6. It's theirs.
7. They're theirs.
8. It's his.
9. They're theirs.
10. It's ours.

I'm Looking for a Jacket

B. (Page 157)
1. a jacket
2. blue

C. (Page 157)
Sales clerk: Can I help you?
Nadia: Yes. I'm looking for a jacket.
Sales clerk: These jackets are **on** special. We're having a sale.
Nadia: Oh, I like this one. Does it come **in** blue?
Sales clerk: No, it only **comes** in black.
Nadia: Well, thanks anyway.
Sales clerk: You**'re** welcome.

What Are You Doing Today?

B. (Page 157)
1. cleaning her house
2. relaxing

C. (Page 158)
Yumi: Hi Lili. **What's** up? Are you busy today?
Lili: A little bit. I'm cleaning my house. How about you?
Yumi: Oh, I'm relaxing today. **Right** now I'm drinking coffee and reading the newspaper.
Lili: Maybe we can **get** together later.
Yumi: Sure. That **sounds** good. I'll call you later.
Lili: 'Bye.

Unit 13

Words You Need (Page 164)
1. a
2. h
3. i
4. f
5. e
6. b

7. c
8. j
9. g
10. k
11. d

Understand: Past Continuous Aspect

A. (Page 166)
1. Yumi
2. Anne
3. Roberto
4. Yumi
5. Yumi and Anne
6. Max
7. Chen
8. Joseph
9. Nadia and Carla
10. Carla

B. (Page 167)
1. Tom wasn't asking for directions
2. Anne wasn't carrying a newspaper.
3. Yumi wasn't wearing her raincoat.
4. Ali and Chen weren't going to the bank.
5. We weren't sitting in the bus.
6. Lili wasn't speaking to me.
7. Max wasn't waiting for us at the hotel.
8. Roberto wasn't looking for Nadia.
9. They weren't staying in an old hotel.
10. Nadia wasn't studying Spanish.

Understand: Adverbs of Manner

A. (Page 168)

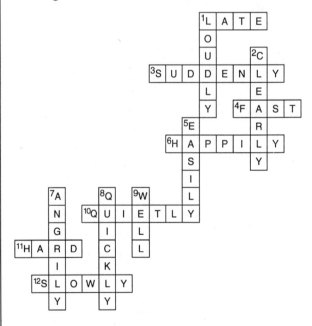

B. (Page 168)
1. quiet
2. slowly
3. loudly
4. badly
5. quiet
6. hard
7. well
8. nicely
9. late
10. good

Understand: Question Words "How" and "Why"

A. (Page 169)

1. clearly	5. carefully
2. loudly	6. hard
3. happily	7. fast
4. quietly	8. hungrily

B. (Page 169)

1. e	5. c
2. d	6. g
3. b	7. a
4. h	8. f

C. (Page 170)
1. 3:00 a.m.
2. quietly
3. at a door
4. a person snoring loudly
5. a special key
6. a wallet
7. into his pocket
8. He got into his car and drove away.
9. smiling happily

Understand: Object Pronouns

A. (Page 171)

1. him	6. us
2. her	7. I
3. They	8. I
4. me	9. We
5. them	10. us

B. (Page 172)

1. us	6. her
2. They	7. us
3. it	8. They
4. It	9. him
5. them	10. it

What Were You Doing Yesterday?

B. (Page 172)

1. at home	3. old movies
2. watching TV	

C. (Page 172)
Carla: Where were you yesterday?
Yumi: I was at home.
Carla: **What** were you doing?
Yumi: **Not** much. I was watching TV.
Carla: Was there anything good on TV?
Yumi: **Not** really. I was watching old movies.
Carla: I **love** old movies.
Yumi: Me too.

How Was the Party?

B. (Page 173)
1. at a party
2. No one was dancing or talking.

C. (Page 173)
Tom: Where were you last night?
Joseph: I was at **a** party.
Tom: **How** was it?
Joseph: Pretty boring.
Tom: How **come**?
Joseph: No one was dancing. No one was talking. I left early.
Tom: Oh, that's too **bad**.

Unit 14

Understand: "Will" for Future Time

A. (Page 179)
1. It will snow in Toronto in January.
2. I will visit my parents at Thanksgiving.
3. She will eat dinner at 8:00.
4. It will be on TV at six o'clock.
5. They will eat dinner in a restaurant.
6. We will go to the beach in the morning.
7. I will be here for the English exam.
8. He will come home at six o'clock.
9. They will take a walk near the beach.
10. You will watch the news on TV.

B. (Page 180)

1. help	7. 'll bring
2. 'll talk	8. 'll tell
3. 'll be	9. 'll play
4. 'll say	10. 'll meet
5. 'll come	11. 'll call
6. 'll cook	

Understand: "Will" for Future Time, Question Form

A. (Page 181)
1. Will Tom and Ali be here soon?
2. Will Anne go back to work next week?
3. Will you help me find my glasses?
4. Will he telephone you tomorrow?
5. Will she carry it for you?
6. Will Roberto send us copies of the picture?
7. Will the car start in cold weather?
8. Will Nadia and Carla choose the restaurant?
9. Will Max study English in Florida?
10. Will the bus take us to the airport?

B. (Page 181)

1.	b	6.	e
2.	i	7.	j
3.	g	8.	d
4.	a	9.	h
5.	c	10.	f

Understand: "Will" for Future Time Negative

A. (Page 182)
1. He won't pass the exam.
2. That bus won't leave on time.
3. He won't call his friend tomorrow.
4. They won't tell us about it.
5. I won't go out in the rain.
6. She won't remember to phone tonight.
7. You won't be cold with that coat.
8. We won't be home tonight.
9. The train won't arrive on time.
10. It won't rain on the weekend.

B. (Page 182)

1.	Yes, it will.	6.	No, it won't.
2.	Yes, they will.	7.	No, they won't.
3.	Yes, it will.	8.	Yes, they will.
4.	No, they won't.	9.	No, they won't.
5.	No, they won't.	10.	Yes, it will.

Understand: "Be Going To" for Future Plans

A. (Page 184)
1. Anne is going to go to bed at 11 o'clock.
2. Roberto is going to take a taxi on Mondays.
3. They are going to go to movies on the weekend.
4. We are going to watch the news on TV.
5. Max is going to be late for work today.
6. I am going to go to bed early on Sunday nights.
7. The store is going to close at five o'clock today.
8. Nadia and Yumi are going to play tennis near the hotel.
9. Joseph is going to ask the tour guide for information.
10. Tom and Ali are going to take pictures of the group.

B. (Page 184)

1.	going to go	6.	Correct
2.	Correct	7.	Correct
3.	is going to play	8.	is going to wait
4.	Correct	9.	am going to eat
5.	are going to buy	10.	is going to rain

Understand: "Be Going To" Negative

A. (Page 185)
1. They aren't going to meet us downstairs.
2. You aren't going to watch TV.
3. She isn't going to forget her purse.
4. I'm not going to tell him.
5. We aren't going to stay in this hotel.
6. They aren't going to play tennis today.
7. He isn't going to eat an orange.
8. You aren't going to need an umbrella.
9. I'm not going to stay up late.
10. She isn't going to cook dinner tonight.

B. (Page 185)

1.	not	6.	am
2.	going	7.	going
3.	is	8.	to
4.	to	9.	not
5.	not	10.	to

Understand: "Be Going To" Question Form

A. (Page 186)
1. Is Tom going to go downtown?
2. Are Yumi and Carla going to meet later?
3. Is it going to rain tonight?
4. Are we going to enjoy that movie?
5. Is Roberto going to take the bus?
6. Are they going to take a taxi?
7. Is Anne going to buy stamps?
8. Is Chen going to drive there?
9. Are Max and Ali going to drink coffee?
10. Is Nadia going to phone you later?

B. (Page 187)

1.	b	5.	a
2.	f	6.	e
3.	g	7.	d
4.	c		

Understand: Expressions of Future time (Page 187)

1.	a	5.	b
2.	g	6.	d
3.	c	7.	f
4.	e		

Understand: Prepositions of Direction and Position (Page 188)

1.	Ø	6.	to
2.	at	7.	Ø
3.	to	8.	at
4.	to	9.	to
5.	at	10.	Ø

What Are You Going to Do on the Weekend?

B. (Page 189)
1. sleep in
2. No, he isn't.
3. take his car to the garage

C. (Page 190)

Tom: What are you doing on the weekend?

Max: Well, on Saturday morning I'm going to sleep **in**.

Tom: Are you going to play tennis Saturday afternoon?

Max: Nah. I'm going to take it **easy** all day. How about you? **Any** plans for Saturday?

Tom: I'm going to take my car to the garage in the morning. After that, **who** knows?

This Is a Friend of Mine

B. (Page 190)

1. Yumi's friend   2. in Vancouver

C. (Page 190)

Yumi: Tom, do you know my friend Keiko?

Tom: No, I don't. Can you introduce us?

Yumi: Sure. Come on **over**. I'll introduce you. Keiko, meet Tom. He's a friend of **mine**.

Keiko: Nice to meet you, Tom.

Yumi: Tom, meet Keiko. she's going to study English in Vancouver.

Tom: **Nice** to meet you, Keiko.

Unit 15

Count and Non-Count Nouns

A. (Page 193)

1.	any	6.	any
2.	some	7.	any
3.	some	8.	some
4.	any	9.	any
5.	any	10.	any

B. (Page 193)

1.	There is	6.	There is
2.	There is	7.	Is there
3.	Is there	8.	There is
4.	There are	9.	There isn't
5.	There are	10.	Is there

Present Continuous

A. (Page 194)

1.	Yumi and Carla	6.	Lili and Nadia
2.	Roberto	7.	Joseph
3.	Max	8.	Carla
4.	Anne	9.	Tom
5.	Chen	10.	Yumi

B. (Page 194)

1.	Joseph is	6.	a map
2.	a newspaper	7.	Nadia is
3.	near Nadia and Lili	8.	Lili is
4.	tea	9.	the tour guide is
5.	Max is	10.	in a cafe

C. (Page 195)

1.	sitting	6.	playing
2.	speaking	7.	buying
3.	carrying	8.	wearing
4.	eating	9.	planning
5.	taking	10.	drinking

D. (Page 195)

Possible answers:

Friday Night

1. Lili is drinking tea.
2. Nadia is reading a book.
3. Roberto is taking a picture.
4. Max is eating cake.
5. Chen is talking to Max.
6. Lili and Carla are talking.
7. Yumi is serving drinks.
8. Chen is wearing a jacket.
9. Lili is wearing a dress.
10. Roberto is wearing a sweater and pants.
11. Nadia and Joseph are sitting on a couch.
12. Joseph is listening to music.

Saturday night

1. Anne is playing the piano.
2. Roberto is playing the guitar.
3. Carla is sitting on the floor.
4. Yumi is serving cookies.
5. Max is eating cookies.
6. Chen is drinking coffee.
7. Joseph is talking to Tom.
8. Tom is taking a picture.
9. Chen is wearing a sweater.
10. Carla is wearing jeans.
11. Yumi is wearing a dress.
12. Joseph and Tom are sitting on the couch.

E. (Page 196)

Possible answers:

1. On Friday night, Yumi was serving drinks. On Saturday night, Yumi was serving cookies.
2. On Friday night, Joseph was listening to music. On Saturday night, Joseph was talking to Tom.
3. On Friday night, Lili was there. On Saturday night, she wasn't.
4. On Friday night, Carla was talking to Lili. On Saturday night, Carla was listening to music.
5. On Friday night, Roberto was taking pictures. On Saturday night, Tom was taking pictures.
6. On Friday night, Max was eating cake. On Saturday night, Max was eating cookies.
7. On Friday night, Nadia and Joseph were sitting on the couch. On Saturday night, Tom and Joseph were sitting on the couch.
8. On Friday night, Nadia was there, but Tom wasn't. On Saturday night, Tom was there, but Nadia wasn't.

9. On Friday night, Yumi was wearing a T-shirt and pants. On Saturday night, Yumi was wearing a dress.

Past Continuous
Adverbs of Manner

A. (Page 196)
1. badly
2. carefully
3. quickly
4. fast
5. slowly
6. suddenly
7. happily
8. hard
9. rapidly
10. easily

B. (Page 196)
1. in a taxi
2. hard
3. fast
4. He wasn't wearing is seat belt. He fell.
5. in an ambulance
6. on a bed
7. questions
8. the doctor
9. because the doctor wasn't coming quickly
10. a shot

Future with "Be Going To"

A. (Page 196)
1. have a party for Yumi's birthday
2. bring a birthday cake
3. a birthday present
4. play music
5. because her friends are going to surprise her
6. because they don't want to be tired in the morning
7. tomorrow morning
8. at the airport
9. by taxi
10. early

B. (Page 197)
1. Where are we going to go?
2. What is Anne going to bring?
3. What are Lili and Carla going to shop for?
4. What are Roberto and Max going to do?
5. What are Yumi's friends going to do?
6. Who isn't going to stay long?
7. When is Nadia's sister going to arrive?
8. Where are they going to meet her?
9. When are they going to go to bed?
10. What are they going to use?

Lista Mexic

Mami & Tati	Matty & Luke

Mami & Tati

- 3 yoga mats
- 2 slipi tati

Matty & Luke

- DVD player + DVD-uri
  1 - wall-e
  2 - madagascar
  3 - ice age
  4 - sponge bob
  5 -

- rice cereal - 1 box
- lapte praf
- suzete
- biberoane
- sticle de apă - sippy cups
- bandane / baticuțe / șepcă
- săcunelul vibrat
-